Advancing Responsible Adolescent Development

Series Editor
Roger J.R. Levesque
Indiana University, Bloomington, IN, U.S.A

For further volumes:
http://www.springer.com/series/7284

Stephen T. Russell · Lisa J. Crockett · Ruth K. Chao
Editors

Asian American Parenting and Parent-Adolescent Relationships

Springer

Editors
Stephen T. Russell
Norton School of Family
and Consumer Sciences
University of Arizona
Tucson, AZ 85721
strussell@arizona.edu

Lisa J. Crockett
Department of Psychology
University of Nebraska-Lincoln
Lincoln, NE 68588
ecrockett1@unl.edu

Ruth K. Chao
Department of Psychology
University of California, Riverside
Riverside, CA 92521
ruth.chao@ucr.edu

ISBN 978-1-4419-5727-6 e-ISBN 978-1-4419-5728-3
DOI 10.1007/978-1-4419-5728-3
Springer New York Dordrecht Heidelberg London

Library of Congress Control Number: 2010920316

Printed on acid-free paper

Springer is part of Springer Science+Business Media (www.springer.com)

Preface

The relationships between children and their parents are the building blocks for family relationships throughout life. The nature of the parent-child relationship begins with parenting—the practices and strategies that parents engage in as they raise their children. Parenting during childhood sets the stage for parent-adolescent relationships. These relationships make a critical difference during the teenage years: we know that when parent-adolescent relationships are healthy and strong, adolescents are more likely to have high aspirations and achievement, and to make healthier choices when it comes to risk-taking.

Most of the research in this field has been based in the United States and has been conducted through studies of European American families. Yet a growing body of research suggests important ethnic differences in styles of parenting and the qualities characterizing the parent-adolescent relationship. In this area of research, most existing studies have examined ethnic and cultural group differences using widely accepted measures and concepts of parenting. Comparative studies assume that dimensions of parenting such as parental warmth or control have the same meaning across cultures; however, given that conceptualizations of adolescent-parent relationships have been developed and tested on samples comprised largely of European Americans, we cannot rule out the possibility that the way we understand parenting has been shaped by the predominantly Western- and U.S.-focused research in this field. Thus, the meanings of relationship qualities that underlie parenting practices and parenting styles in other ethnic/racial populations have rarely been examined, and there is little basis for knowing how well parenting constructs apply in other racial/ethnic groups.

Although most of the existing research has been based in the United States and has typically focused on European American families, it is also the case that, due to the growing numbers of non-European Americans in the United States, there are strategic opportunities to study the cultural basis of parenting practices and parent-adolescent relationships. For this book, the emphasis on Asian American parenting and parent-adolescent relationships is rooted in two important trends. First, at the population level, Asian Americans are among the fastest growing ethnic groups in the United States. Within this broad ethnic group are diverse ethnic subgroups that, while sharing an Asian cultural origin, have very distinct subcultural identities and histories that have shaped the nature and dynamics of family life. We focus on Chinese and Filipino Americans in this book, the two largest Asian American ethnic groups in the United States. Further, they are two groups that share Asian cultural heritage yet have distinct histories of Western cultural influence in their respective countries of origin: the historical cultural separation and independence of China has had notably different implications for the culture of family life when compared to the Western colonization of the Philippines. Further, these two ethnic groups have had different histories of immigration to the United States, which have led to differences in their U.S. immigrant experiences.

The second relevant trend that led to this study of Asian American family relationships has been a trend in research. A growing number of studies have shown that there are distinctive cultural processes for the family socialization of Asian Americans. In particular, in the last decade, studies have shown that the two dimensions of parenting that have been held to be fundamental—warmth and control—have distinctly different relevance and meaning from the perspective of Asian American culture. Based on this work, a focus on Asian Americans—and the distinctiveness of Chinese versus Filipino American family life—is strategic for new research that may illuminate the cultural underpinnings of parenting and parent-adolescent relationships.

Thus, the goal of this book is to bring together a diverse group of studies of Asian Americans and their families that, taken together, can tell a new story about the cultural basis for parenting and parent-adolescent relationships. This book draws from complementary sources of data to contribute to the understanding of measures, meanings, and cultural beliefs about Asian American parenting and parent-adolescent relationships. We include (1) a large, nationally representative survey of adolescents' relationships with their parents; (2) a survey study of adolescents and their parents designed to investigate cultural differences in parenting between Asian immigrants and European Americans; (3) a survey study designed to compare the experiences of Chinese and Filipino American adolescents; and (4) a qualitative study that investigates parent-adolescent relationships from the perspective of contemporary Asian American adolescents.

Our results highlight the contributions that can be made by applying multiple research methods; we show that different methods provide distinct but complementary insights for understanding cultural differences in parent-adolescent relationships. We point out differences between European, Chinese, and Filipino Americans, and show that understandings of parenting vary by ethnicity but also for adolescent females compared to males, and for relationships with mothers compared to fathers. Thus, in addition to contributing to the growing body of research on ethnicity and parenting, our study advances understandings of ethnic diversity in contemporary parenting behaviors and adolescent-parent relationships.

Acknowledgments

This research was funded by grants HD R01 039438 from the National Institute of Child Health and Human Development to L. Crockett and S. Russell and HD R01 38949-02 from the National Institute of Child Health and Human Development to R. Chao. For Chapter 2, we owe special thanks to George Knight for his methodological consultation and to Yuh-Ling Shen and Davood Tofighi for their assistance in data analysis. For Chapters 5 and 6 we thank Faye C. H. Lee for her methodological consultation and assistance in data analysis and interpretation.

In part, this research uses data from Add Health, a program project designed by J. Richard Udry, Peter S. Bearman, and Kathleen Mullan Harris, and funded by a grant P01-HD31921 from the National Institute of Child Health and Human Development, with cooperative funding from 17 other agencies. Special acknowledgment is due Ronald R. Rindfuss and Barbara Entwisle for assistance in the original design. Persons interested in obtaining data files from Add Health should contact Add Health, Carolina Population Center, 123 W. Franklin Street, Chapel Hill, NC 27516-2524 (www.cpc.unc.edu/addhealth/contract.html).

Tucson, AZ Stephen T. Russell

Contents

1 **Introduction: Asian American Parenting and Parent-Adolescent Relationships** 1
Stephen T. Russell, Lisa J. Crockett, and Ruth K. Chao

2 **Do Measures of Parenting Have the Same Meaning for European, Chinese, and Filipino American Adolescents? Tests of Measurement Equivalence** 17
Lisa J. Crockett, Glen J. Veed, and Stephen T. Russell

3 **Parental Beliefs and Their Relation to the Parental Practices of Immigrant Chinese Americans and European Americans** 37
Inna A. Padmawidjaja and Ruth K. Chao

4 **Parental Sacrifice and Acceptance as Distinct Dimensions of Parental Support Among Chinese and Filipino American Adolescents** 61
Ruth K. Chao and Kevin F. Kaeochinda

5 **The Meanings of Parent-Adolescent Relationship Quality Among Chinese American and Filipino American Adolescents** . . . 79
Stephen T. Russell, June Y. Chu, Lisa J. Crockett, and Stacey N. Doan

6 **Interdependent Independence: The Meanings of Autonomy Among Chinese American and Filipino American Adolescents** . . . 101
Stephen T. Russell, June Y. Chu, Lisa J. Crockett, and Sun-A Lee

7 **Conclusions: The Role of Asian American Culture in Parenting and Parent-Adolescent Relationships** 117
Stephen T. Russell, Lisa J. Crockett, and Ruth K. Chao

Subject Index 129

Contributors

Ruth K. Chao University of California, Riverside, CA, USA, ruth.chao@ucr.edu

June Y. Chu University of Pennsylvania, Philadelphia, PA, USA, jychu@pobox.upenn.edu

Lisa J. Crockett University of Nebraska, Lincoln, NE, USA, ecrockett1@unl.edu

Stacey N. Doan Cornell University, Ithaca, NY, USA, sbd9@cornell.edu

Kevin F. Kaeochinda University of California, Riverside, CA, USA, kkaeo001@ucr.edu

Sun-A Lee Georgia Southern University, Statesboro, GA, USA, sunalee@georgiasouthern.edu

Inna A. Padmawidjaja University of California, Riverside, CA, USA, innapad@gmail.com

Stephen T. Russell University of Arizona, Tucson, AZ, USA, strussell@arizona.edu

Glen J. Veed University of Nebraska, Lincoln, NE, USA, veed@huskers.unl.edu

About the Authors

Stephen T. Russell is Professor and Fitch Nesbitt Endowed Chair in Family and Consumer Sciences in the John & Doris Norton School of Family and Consumer Sciences at the University of Arizona, and Director of the Frances McClelland Institute for Children, Youth, and Families. He completed his Ph.D. in Sociology at Duke University in 1994 and postdoctoral training in Life Course Studies at UNC-Chapel Hill in 1997. Stephen conducts research on adolescent pregnancy and parenting, cultural influences on parent-adolescent relationships, and the health and development of sexual minority youth. With Dr. Lisa Crockett he has been involved in a multi-year study of cross-cultural parenting and adolescent adjustment. He received a Wayne F. Placek Award from the American Psychological Foundation (2000), was a William T. Grant Foundation Scholar (2001–2006), a board member of the National Council on Family Relations (2005–2008), and was elected as a member of the International Academy of Sex Research in 2004. He is Associate Editor for the *Journal for Research on Adolescence.*

Lisa J. Crockett is Professor of Psychology at the University of Nebraska-Lincoln. She received her Ph.D. from the University of Chicago in 1986 and completed post-doctoral training at the Johns Hopkins School of Public Health. She was also a faculty member in the Department of Human Development and Family Studies at the Pennsylvania State University. Lisa conducts research in two primary areas: adolescent risk behavior, with an emphasis on sexuality, and ethnic differences in parenting and adolescent adjustment. In collaboration with Dr. Russell she has examined the relations between parenting practices and adolescent adjustment across different ethnic groups, using national survey data and qualitative data from focus group interviews with teenagers. Dr. Crockett served as Associate Editor of the *Journal of Research on Adolescence* from 1999 to 2004 and is on the editorial board of the *Journal of Early Adolescence.*

Ruth K. Chao is an Associate Professor in the Department of Psychology at the University of California, Riverside. She received her Ph.D. from University of California, Los Angeles. Dr. Chao was also an Assistant Professor in the Department of Child and Family Studies at Syracuse University. Her research interests include socio-cultural perspectives of parenting and the family, focusing on

Asian immigrants. She recently completed a 5-year longitudinal study, funded by the National Institute of Health, examining the effects of parental control, warmth, and parental involvement in school on adolescents' school performance and behavioral adjustment. Her research also includes studies of the language acculturation of Asian immigrant families across time and its effects on adolescents' adjustment.

June Y. Chu, Ph.D., Director, Pan-Asian American Community House, University of Pennsylvania, received her Ph.D. in Social Psychology from the University of California, Davis (2004). Her research and teaching interests focus upon Asian American well-being and mental health.

Stacey N. Doan is a Ph.D. student in Human Development at Cornell University. She studies cross-cultural differences in parenting and their effects on children's social-emotional outcomes.

Kevin F. Kaeochinda is a Ph.D. student in Psychology at the University of California, Riverside. He studies the cultural bases of parenting.

Sun-A Lee is Assistant Professor in the Department of Hospitality, Tourism, and Family & Consumer Sciences, Georgia Southern University. She completed her Ph.D. in Family Studies and Human Development at the University of Arizona in 2007. Her research focuses on family interaction, family diversity, and adolescents' psychosocial development.

Glen J. Veed, M.A., is a graduate student at the University of Nebraska-Lincoln completing his Ph.D. in Clinical Psychology. He received his Bachelor's degree in Psychology with a minor in Mathematics from the University of Illinois at Urbana-Champaign. His research focuses on measurement development and the influence of the adolescent peer group on the development of psychopathology.

Inna Artati Padmawidjaja completed her Ph.D. at the University of Rochester in 1999. Her research interest is in the area of motivational and emotional development of early childhood, school age, and early adulthood and how developmental processes as well as mental and physical health are affected by contextual factors including ethnic, gender, cultural, and religious beliefs and values.

Chapter 1
Introduction: Asian American Parenting and Parent-Adolescent Relationships

Stephen T. Russell, Lisa J. Crockett, and Ruth K. Chao

A large research literature points to the importance of parenting practices as strong predictors of adolescent psychosocial adjustment (Parke & Buriel, 2006). Much of this research has been shaped by the literature on parenting styles (Baumrind, 1968), work that has provided the foundation for present-day researchers who study parenting practices and parent-child relationships. These parenting styles have been strongly linked to a broad range of indicators of adjustment during the adolescent years, including academic achievement, conduct problems, health and risk behavior (such as smoking, substance use or abuse, and even nutritious dietary habits), and emotional health (including self-esteem and depression). Parental support and control are two key parenting practices that predict adolescent adjustment and serve as the primary dimensions of the now well-known conceptualization of parenting styles (Baumrind, 1991; Maccoby & Martin, 1983). Authoritative parenting, which combines high warmth and sensitivity to an adolescent's needs (support) with firm standards for behavior (control), is associated with this broad range of indicators of well-being during adolescence (Baumrind, 1991; Lamborn, Mounts, Steinberg, & Dornbusch, 1991).

Chao's seminal works (1994, 2001) that compared the parenting styles of European Americans and Asian Americans were the beginning of an emerging body of evidence that documents ethnic differences in the effects of parenting style, which are rooted in cultural meanings ascribed to parenthood and parenting. This work challenges the universality of theories of socialization (Parke & Buriel, 2006); the nature and consequences of parenting styles and parenting practices may vary considerably across ethnic groups due to differences in cultural understandings of parenting (Chao, 1994, 2001; Deater-Deckard, Dodge, Bates, & Pettit, 1996; Lansford et al., 2004). In this book, culture is regarded as a source of meaning that is comprised of broader level folk theories and beliefs, and more specific "scripts"

S.T. Russell (✉)
University of Arizona, Tucson, AZ, USA
e-mail: strussell@arizona.edu

S.T. Russell et al. (eds.), *Asian American Parenting and Parent-Adolescent Relationships*, Advancing Responsible Adolescent Development,
DOI 10.1007/978-1-4419-5728-3_1,

for defining the types of practices parents use or what should be expected of parents (Gallimore, Goldenberg, & Weisner, 1993).

In this book we present a series of studies that investigate the meanings of parenting practices and parenting styles in Asian American families. We focus on Asian American parent-adolescent relationships because prior research suggests distinctive cultural processes for the family socialization of Asian Americans; in addition, Asian Americans are among the fastest growing ethnic groups in the United States. Through the use of four distinct data sources and diverse methodological approaches we examine (1) the equivalence of survey measures of parenting for Asian and European American adolescents, (2) cultural differences in parental beliefs and their relation to parenting practices among European American and Asian American parents of adolescents, (3) a conceptualization of parental support that includes the dimension of sacrifice, empirically tested with two Asian American ethnic subgroups, and (4) the understandings of parental support and autonomy-granting expressed by Asian American adolescent boys and girls.

This chapter provides an overview of current thinking about parent-adolescent relationships and parenting in adolescence. We begin with a discussion of *parental support or warmth* and *parental control*, the two central dimensions that have guided conceptualizations of parenting for decades. We then discuss the role of ethnicity and culture in shaping parenting practices and behaviors; much of that research was developed from studies of Chinese American parents and adolescents. We delve more deeply into the cultural meanings of parenting in Asian American families, including the distinctive roles of mothers and fathers. With that background, we then consider ethnic group differences among Asian Americans in the United States, focusing on Chinese and Filipino American cultural histories and available evidence about cultural variation in parenting and parent-adolescent relationships between these groups. Finally, we close with a detailed outline of the chapters that follow.

Parenting Practices and Adolescent Adjustment

Parenting practices, especially support and control, have emerged as important determinants of children's psychosocial adjustment (Barber, Stolz, & Olsen, 2005; Maccoby & Martin, 1983; Parke & Buriel, 2006). Each has been linked to adolescents' psychological and behavioral adjustment in research with White and multi-ethnic samples (Barrera et al., 2002; Collins & Steinberg, 2006; Conger, Conger, Elder, & Lorenz, 1992; Taylor, Casten, & Flikinger, 1993; Taylor & Roberts, 1995). Supportive parenting, which is characterized by warmth, acceptance, and involvement, tends to be associated with psychological well-being (Barber et al., 2005; Conger & Conger, 1993; Kurdek & Fine, 1994; Ge, Best, Conger, & Simons, 1996). In contrast, non-supportive parenting is associated with lower self-esteem, more depressive symptoms, conduct problems, and psychological disorders (e.g., Conger et al., 1992; Ge et al., 1996; Knight, Virdin, Ocampo, & Roosa, 1994; McLoyd, 1990).

Studies based on European American samples (as well as popular media images) have stressed the *support or warmth* dimension of the parent-adolescent relationship as being the most advantageous for adolescent health and adjustment. Behaviors such as kissing, hugging, praising, and complimenting have been understood to be evidence of high parental warmth and acceptance (Rohner, 1986). Hostility, aggression, indifference, and neglect have historically been considered the opposite extreme, leading to feelings of rejection in the child, as well as negative well-being. Only recently have scholars suggested that the construct of parental support may have dimensions in addition to warmth or acceptance. Specifically, among Asian or immigrant Americans, parental sacrifice is an under-explored dimension that may be central to parental support for some cultural groups (Chao, 1994).

In addition, researchers interested in the family processes underlying adolescents' development have demonstrated that *parental control* has an important influence on adolescents' adjustment and competence. Behavioral control involves regulating children's behaviors through the consistent enforcement of rules or expectations for behavior and through monitoring youth. Although by adolescence parents' use of control may diminish, researchers conclude that moderate behavioral control remains beneficial for child and adolescent development (Baumrind, 1991; Maccoby & Martin, 1983). Behavioral control in the form of parental monitoring and joint parent-child decision making is associated with lower rates of externalizing problems (substance use and delinquency; Dornbusch, 1985; Jacobson & Crockett, 2000) and with higher levels of academic achievement (Barber, Olsen, & Shagle, 1994; Mason, Cauce, & Gonzales, 1997; Steinberg, Elmen, & Mounts, 1989; Stice & Barrera, 1995). Moderate behavioral control may also be beneficial for adolescents' emotional well-being. Other studies have also found that behavioral control by parents was associated with fewer adolescent internalizing problems, and specifically with decreases in adolescents' depressed affect (Barber et al., 1994; Jacobson & Crockett, 2000). This type of control has been distinguished from *psychological control*, which is more manipulative and guilt-based, involving control over the child's psychological world, and is associated with higher rates of internalizing problems (e.g., depression), as well as delinquency and school misconduct (Barber & Harmon, 2002; Barber et al., 1994). However, control that restricts adolescents' sense of psychological autonomy is associated with increased internalizing symptoms (Barber et al., 1994, 2005). Thus, moderate behavioral control deters problem behavior and may enhance adolescents' psychological well-being, but overly strict or intrusive control can be psychologically debilitating.

Ethnicity, Culture, and Parenting

The large research literature on parenting styles has historically been based on studies of European American, middle-class families and has been criticized for its ethnocentricity (Chao, 1994; Julian, McHenry, & McKelvey, 1994). The formative research by Baumrind (1967) showed that authoritative parents—defined by a combination of high parental responsiveness, warmth, behavioral supervision and strictness, and democracy—generally had children with little anxiety or insecurity who did well in school. Since then, additional studies have found that the authoritative style is beneficial for other ethnic groups, but not necessarily more beneficial than authoritarian parenting. For example, when Dornbusch, Ritter, Leiderman, Roberts, and Fraleigh (1987) asked Asian American students to rate their parents, they discovered that these students often rated their parents as authoritarian (authoritarian parents show high levels of parental demands, low levels of parental responsiveness, and high levels of parental control). Paradoxically, they found that while Asian American students were likely to come from "authoritarian" homes, they showed high levels of academic achievement, despite the fact that this type of parenting had been shown to be non-adaptive in most studies of European American children. Subsequently, Chao (2001) has shown that among first-generation Chinese families, youth from authoritarian homes do just as well in school as those from authoritative homes.

There is some evidence that the prevalence of particular parenting practices differs across ethnic groups (Shumow & Lomax, 2002; Steinberg, Lamborn, Darling, & Mounts, 1994). For example, in a large multi-ethnic sample, 25% of white intact middle-class families, but only 14–16% of comparable Black, Hispanic, and Asian American families were classified as authoritative based on adolescents' reports (Steinberg, Mounts, Lamborn, & Dornbusch, 1991). A number of studies have focused attention on ethnic group differences in levels of parental control: Asian American, African American, and Latino parents all tend to report higher levels of strictness and physical discipline than European Americans (Chao, 1994; Lin & Fu, 1990; Deater-Deckard et al., 1996; Lansford et al., 2004; Dornbusch et al., 1987; Hill, 2001; Pinderhughes, Dodge, Bates, Pettit, & Zelli, 2000; Pinderhughes, Nix, Foster, & Jones, 2001). Studies of parenting style indicate that Asian parents may be more authoritarian than European American parents. In one study Asian, African American, and Hispanic families received higher scores than Whites on an index of authoritarian parenting, which couples low supportiveness with high control (Dornbusch et al., 1987). Because authoritative and authoritarian parents differ primarily in their expression of warmth/supportiveness, it is possible that Asian American parents display lower warmth as measured in these studies. Asian parents may also be more controlling and restrictive. Chinese American parents in particular have been found to use more restrictive parenting practices and to exert more control in comparison to European American parents (Chiu, 1987; Lin & Fu, 1990). Less is known about other Asian groups.

What is the basis for these observed patterns of ethnic group differences in parenting behaviors and their effects on adolescent adjustment? Ethnic differences in parenting may stem from cultural differences in the meaning of particular parenting practices. Chao's influential work (1994) questioned the applicability of the label "authoritarian" to Asian American families, arguing that many Asian immigrant parents feel that control is not only necessary, but an important responsibility of parents. These higher levels of endorsement and use of parental control among

Asian immigrant parents relative to European American parents may be explained by the different cultural meanings attributed to parenting practices. Authoritarian parenting, as defined by Baumrind (1967), reflects unquestioning obedience to parents along with low levels of parental responsiveness and warmth. However, Chiu (1987) noted that Chinese American mothers were more restrictive than Caucasian mothers, but interpreted their strictness as an attempt to protect children, not inhibit them. Upon closer examination, Chao (1994) discovered that while participants classified their mothers as authoritarian, the ways that Chinese American mothers interacted with their children were qualitatively different from how European American authoritarian mothers interacted with their children. Specifically, the style of parenting used by the Chinese Americans incorporated the indigenous concepts of *chiao shun* and *guan*, which are rooted in Confucian ideology. The Chinese character for guan literally means "to govern" and "to love," and is viewed as parents' responsibility to the child, while the meaning of chiao shun is "to train." A critical part of the parental role is to provide your children with chiao shun or guan. Chinese American parents are not necessarily motivated to dominate their child (as authoritarian parents are apt to do); rather, parents are expected to teach and guide their children so as to maintain harmonious relationships with others. Additionally, parents who chiao shun or guan their children are very involved in their children's lives and show high levels of concern for their offspring. This is the antithesis of authoritarian parenting, whose roots date back to the idea of "breaking the child's will" as a means to overcome the Puritan notion of "original sin" (Chao, 1994).

This expanded, culturally based understanding of Asian parenting suggests that the central dimensions of parenting styles—parental support/warmth and parental control—should have culturally distinct meanings. Parental warmth or responsiveness, particularly parents' emotional demonstrativeness to children, may be interpreted differently by some Asian immigrants in the United States in comparison to European Americans (Chao, 2001; Wu & Chao, 2005). Wu and Chao (2005) found that Chinese American adolescents reported lower levels of parental warmth than their European American counterparts, noting that this finding is consistent with the value placed on self-control and restraint, especially emotional restraint, emphasized throughout Asia. This value is consistent with the Confucian doctrine in which emotion is considered somewhat harmful to one's health and relationships, and therefore should be avoided. As a consequence, Asian American parents do not typically express affection and warmth openly. Instead, Asian parents demonstrate their love and affection through their instrumental support and sacrifice, especially with regard to their children's education. Asian American immigrant parents assure the welfare of their children not only by meeting their daily needs, but through the sacrifices that, for many, motivated migration (Chao & Tseng, 2002; Fuligni & Yoshikawa, 2002). In contrast to Asian norms of parental warmth, mainstream American culture advocates more direct or expressive communication, and thus relies on more demonstrative expressions of parental love and affection, such as hugging, kissing, and praising children.

The other primary dimension of parenting—control—may be interpreted by Asian immigrant families as parental concern and care rather than as hostility and rejection, which are the associations often made by European American adolescents (Chao, 1994). Although among adolescents in North America and Germany parental control was found to be associated with perceived parental hostility and rejection (Nomura, Noguchi, Saito, & Tezuka, 1995; Trommsdorff, 1985), the same control behaviors were associated with perceived parental warmth and acceptance among adolescents in Japan, Korea, and mainland China (Kornadt, 1987; Lau & Cheung, 1987; Lau et al., 1990; Nomura et al., 1995; Rohner & Petengill, 1985; Trommsdorff, 1985). In fact, Japanese adolescents feel *rejected* when their parents exercise little control (Trommsdorff, 1985). In Chinese American culture, strictness and control are linked to proper parental care and concern. Thus, practices that appear overly restrictive or critical to the outside observer may not be perceived negatively by the child but rather as an indicator of concern and support (for related examples, see Gonzales, Cauce, & Mason, 1996; Lansford et al., 2005).

This review suggests that frameworks for understanding parenting that have been historically based on European American culture may miss crucial dimensions that inform parental behaviors and their meanings in other cultural groups. Under these circumstances, the lack of negative effects of strict parenting among Chinese American children and youth would not be surprising. Consistent with this notion, research on parenting style has shown that "authoritarian" practices, although associated with poorer functioning among European American youth, have less detrimental effects among Asian adolescents (Chao, 2001; Steinberg et al., 1994). Chao (2001) directly tested for differences in parenting style effects across European Americans and two generations of Chinese Americans by estimating interaction effects for ethnicity and parenting style. She found for European Americans, more so than for first-generation Chinese, youth with authoritative parents did better in school than those with authoritarian parents. Among first-generation Chinese, youth from authoritarian homes did just as well in school as those from authoritative homes. Steinberg and colleagues (1994) also estimated interaction effects for ethnicity and parenting style; they noted that authoritative parenting had more beneficial consequences for European American youth than for Asian American youth, whereas authoritarian parenting had more positive consequences for Asian American youth compared to their European American counterparts. Thus, even in direct tests *across* groups, the meaning (and consequences) of certain parenting practices may differ across cultural contexts. Further evidence in support of this interpretation comes from recent cross-cultural work on the use of physical discipline. Using samples from six countries, Lansford and her colleagues (2005) found that although use of physical discipline was positively associated with externalizing behavior in all samples, the strength of the association varied depending on the degree to which physical discipline was perceived as normative. Thus, in countries where children viewed physical discipline as normal, the association with externalizing behavior was weaker. This work highlights the role of cultural norms in modulating the effects of parental behavior.

Asian American Culture and Maternal and Paternal Parenting Practices

A small body of research points to gender differences that are relevant for understanding warmth and control in parent-adolescent relationships—both differences between mothers and fathers and differences in the treatment of daughters versus sons. For example, some researchers believe that conflicts with mothers are more common than with fathers, perhaps due to mothers' greater involvement in the daily lives of their adolescent children (Fuligni, 1998; Greenberger & Chen, 1996). Fuligni (1998) found consistent support for this: across four ethnic groups (Mexican, Chinese, Filipino, and European), girls and boys reported low levels of conflict with both parents, but greater conflict with mothers than fathers. On the other hand, Asian American adolescents report more difficulty communicating with parents, particularly fathers, than do European American adolescents (Rhee, Chang, & Rhee, 2003). Chinese American adults in mainland China, Taiwan, and Hong Kong all perceived that mothers are generally warmer and less controlling than fathers (Berndt, Cheung, Lau, & Hau, 1993). Fathers were especially likely to encourage children to be independent and achieve, which coincides with Chinese American beliefs about the control one can exert over one's success. Studies conducted in China have found that fathers have primary responsibility for children's social and school adjustment (Chen, Liu, & Li, 2000). Chinese children report fathers to be more controlling and less warm toward sons than daughters, whereas mothers are reported as more controlling but no less warm toward daughters than toward sons (Berndt et al., 1993). Children in mainland China reported that there were no differences between mothers and fathers on warmth and indulgence for both boys and girls; however, maternal warmth contributed toward later emotional adjustment, whereas paternal warmth predicted later social and school adjustment, including social preference, social competence, aggression disruptiveness, and academic achievement (Chen et al., 2000).

Ethnic Differences Among Asian Americans

In research on cultural variability in parenting practices, much of the attention has been on differences across ethnic groups, although attention to within ethnic group differences may be equally important (Parke & Buriel, 2006). Asian Americans are a large, heterogeneous group. According to Uba (1994), over 25 ethnic groups are encapsulated under the umbrella of "Asian American" in the United States; the two largest Asian American ethnic groups in the United States are Chinese Americans and Filipino Americans (Min, 2006). Most studies of Asian American families have focused on Chinese Americans, although attention to Filipino American populations has grown in recent years. Asian American families have often been characterized as collectivistic in nature, with the interdependence of family members being an important value to instill. Yet the cultural basis of parenting beliefs and parenting practices is likely to vary among Asian American ethnic groups. Parenting in Chinese American families has been traditionally influenced by Confucianism, with its emphasis on respect for authority, filial piety, and the importance of education (Chao & Tseng, 2002). In contrast, Filipino Americans have a long history of Catholicism and Spanish influence, followed by U.S. occupation or colonization until the 1970s. The cultural, historical, and economic differences between these two subgroups could result in differential levels of parental support and control as well as differences in the consequences of these parenting practices for adolescent well-being.

Chinese Americans are characterized by emotional self-control, family recognition through achievement and filial piety, adherence to conformity, and norms of collectivism. Wu (2001) describes parenting as an "ongoing negotiation process for Chinese parents living in the West" (p. 237), as they must consider which aspects of their native culture to maintain, and which new values to adopt. Chinese American parents have been found to be more control oriented (Lin & Fu, 1990), less emotionally expressive (Bond & Wang, 1983; Wu & Chao, 2005), and more restrictive (Chiu, 1987) in comparison to European American parents. Expectations for Chinese American children are high—adolescents are responsible for a range of family functions, including caring for siblings and family members, cleaning the home, and cooking meals (Fuligni, Yip, & Tseng, 2002). Filial duties are stressed in the collective Chinese American family, and a child's responsibility to the family has been shown both empirically and anecdotally to be an accepted norm in Chinese American households (Uba, 1994). Furthermore, children are socialized to maintain harmony with others, and in order to maintain this harmony it becomes important for parents to teach family respect, support, and assistance in the socialization of their children (Fuligni et al., 2002). These practices create the context for "saving face," a value or behavior related to shame that reinforces conformity to family or society expectations for propriety and harmony (Huang, 1994).

Although most research on Asian American adolescents and families has examined East Asian groups, there has been a slow but steady increase in the number of studies that have focused upon Filipino Americans. Filipino American family relationships and households have been characterized as interdependent. Family members depend upon each other for support, and binding relationships are created through reciprocal obligations, referred to as *utang ng loob*. This is a debt of gratitude that you have for others, and it is often not clear when a debt has been fully paid—so the relationship is an ongoing one (Pe-Pua & Protacio-Marcelino, 2000). Families also use *hiya* as a means of creating conformity. To some, hiya refers to shame, which occurs when one fails to meet expectations or acts in ways that meet with disapproval from family members and others. More recent researchers describe hiya as a "sense of propriety" (Pe-Pua & Protacio-Marcelino, 2000). Filipino American families also teach *pakikisama*, which serves to create harmony within groups. Pakikisama refers to getting along with others even if it may conflict with one's own desires. Others have defined this as "smooth interpersonal relations" (Pe-Pua & Protacio-Marcelino, 2000).

A recent study by Fuligni and Pedersen (2002) describes the interdependent character of family culture among young Filipino Americans. Comparing Filipino American, Latin American, East Asian, and European American young adults on family obligations, the study showed that Filipino American and Latin American young adults place the most importance on family obligation. Filipino American young adults were more likely than East Asian young adults to retain their families' traditional emphasis on instrumental help and respect for parents and siblings, even after accounting for differences in family socioeconomic status (family income). These young adults have a strong belief in their role of supporting the family and "remain intimately connected to the daily maintenance of the household" (Fuligni & Pederson, 2002, p. 865). In another cross-cultural study, Filipino mothers described a competent child as one who helps care for younger siblings; this characterization was less frequent by European American or Caribbean mothers (Durbrow, Pena, Masten, Sesma, & Williamson, 2001). Furthermore, in addition to sibling care and household chores, Filipino children are expected to provide for the basic needs of the family (e.g., tuition for siblings' schooling).

These studies show that Filipino Americans' American family life is rooted in culturally distinctive beliefs about reciprocal obligation and interpersonal harmony. The cultural basis of these beliefs can be understood in light of two characteristics of Filipino Americans and families: Filipino Americans are unique in their religious background as they are typically Catholic owing to the Spanish colonization of the Philippines beginning in 1521 (Agbayani-Siewert, 1994), and Filipino Americans are more likely to be egalitarian than patriarchal. First, whereas East Asian cultures have largely been influenced by Confucian and Buddhist philosophies, Filipino American culture has been heavily influenced by Catholicism and Spanish culture. Blair and Qian (1998) have found that Catholicism may also be important in the educational success of Filipino Americans in that Catholicism was positively associated with adolescents' school performance. The further colonization of the Philippines by Americans led to the adoption of the English language in 1898, and the incorporation of many American cultural values.

Second, unlike Confucian-based cultures, Filipino culture does not emphasize patriarchal authority and age stratification as much as East Asian cultures do in that both husband and wife share financial and family decision-making. This greater egalitarianism is consistent with indigenous folk legends that existed prior to Spanish cultural influence (Agbayani-Siewert & Revilla, 1995), including a Filipino creationist legend that both man and woman emerged simultaneously from a large bamboo tube. Sex roles do, however, continue to be strongly influenced by Spanish cultural values. Like the Chinese American, Filipino American women are the primary caretakers of children. Males are socialized to be more aggressive, and the Spanish influence has led to conceptions of "machismo" behaviors (Guthrie & Jacobs, 1966 in Agbayani-Siewert, 1994).

In summary, while Chinese American and Filipino Americans share some Asian cultural values, historical differences in religious, family structure, and immigration traditions point to the possibility of distinct bases for values and beliefs about parenting and parent-adolescent relationships.

New Studies of Asian American Parenting Practices

Dimensions of parenting (warmth and control) are central to understandings of parenting practices and parent-adolescent relationships in multiple cultural settings (Barber et al., 2005). However, the measurement, meanings, and cultural beliefs that underpin these practices have been understudied. Given the distinct cultural bases of Asian and European American parenting, it is plausible that parental behaviors will be interpreted differently by European American, Chinese American, and Filipino American adolescents. Do measures of parenting support and control hold the same cultural meaning for European American and Asian American adolescents, specifically Chinese American and Filipino American adolescents? Are there distinctive dimensions of parental support in addition to warmth and acceptance that have been underexplored in studies which have largely originated from European American scholars and been conducted with European American families? How do adolescents understand or make sense of the support and control provided by their parents? And how do culturally based parental beliefs shape parenting practices? In the chapters that follow we present a series of studies that employ distinct methodological approaches to examine these questions.

In Chapter 2 we consider the role of measurement equivalence in understanding Asian American parenting practices. The ethnic differences reported in existing literatures are difficult to interpret because measures of parenting practices have rarely been validated with Asians. Most measures were initially developed with European American, middle-class samples (Julian et al., 1994), and we do not know whether they assess parenting practices equally well for Asian Americans. Without evidence of measurement equivalence we do not know whether apparent ethnic differences represent true cultural differences in the meanings and consequences of specific parenting practices or whether those differences are simply due to differences in the measurement of key parenting constructs (Knight & Hill, 1998). On a more intuitive level it is important to know how adolescent children perceive and interpret their parents' behavior. Individual parenting practices occur in the context of parent-child relationships (Darling & Steinberg, 1993; Goodnow & Grusec, 1994) and cultural frames of reference (Chao, 1994; Lansford et al., 2005). To begin to address the meaning of parenting practices and parenting measures, we examined adolescents' responses to survey measures of parental support and decision-making autonomy. We relied on standard procedures for establishing measurement equivalence in order to determine whether Chinese American, Filipino American, and European American youth interpret these measures of parenting in similar or in unique ways.

Chapter 3 explores the cultural processes underlying parenting by examining how parental belief systems influence the parenting practices of immigrant Chinese Americans and European Americans. Goodnow and Collins (1990) provide a framework for describing the *content* of parental belief systems that includes parents' goals and their views about the nature of the child, the course of development, and the roles and responsibilities of parents. This chapter focuses on two types of parental goals: those reflecting Confucian notions of child development and learning (e.g., stressing the importance of perseverance, working hard in school, being obedient, and being sensitive to parents' wishes) and a Piagetian and child-centered perspective emphasizing children's self-directed learning and the importance of independence and self-expression. This study includes both adolescents' and parents' reports of parenting in order to capture a family systems perspective which recognizes that adolescents and parents each have their own distinct perceptions of parents' practices. Different types of control are included to reflect the distinctions by Barber et al. (2005) between behavioral control (i.e., monitoring), which has been found to be beneficial for youth, and psychological control (i.e., control over the child's psychological world), which has more deleterious consequences. Additional items for capturing the behavioral control of immigrant Chinese American parents, beyond that of monitoring, are included to capture the Chinese American notion of guan. Thus, cultural "scripts" or expectations for parenting are captured in this study through the broader folk beliefs (i.e., parental belief systems) that inform or shape these scripts for parenting. This study examines not only the extent to which immigrant Chinese American and European Americans practice these three types of parental control, but also how such practices are influenced by their parental belief systems or goals.

The fourth chapter explores parental sacrifice as a central dimension of parental support for Asian American adolescents. With data from a survey study of over 900 high school students, the study involves the exploratory development of a new measure of parental support that includes distinct but closely related dimensions of parental acceptance (or warmth) and sacrifice. Analyses compare Chinese and Filipino American adolescents in order to establish the validity of a measure of parental support that includes sacrifice across these two Asian American ethnic groups. For both ethnic groups, the results affirm the centrality as well as distinctiveness of the construct of sacrifice in the broader notion of parental support. These findings have implications not only for Asian American and immigrant families, but for broadening understandings of all parent-child relationships to include the dimensions of parental sacrifice and associated notions of child obligation, duty, and respect.

Finally, Chapter 5 and Chapter 6 employ qualitative methods to understand Chinese American and Filipino American adolescents' understandings of parental warmth or support Chapter 5 and parental control (conceptualized for the adolescent participants as decision-making autonomy, or independence; Chapter 6). Parenting styles are said to fundamentally reflect the quality of the relationships between parents and children (Darling & Steinberg, 1993; Chao, 2001). However, the meanings of relationship qualities that underlie parenting practices and parenting styles in specific ethnic/racial populations other than European Americans have rarely been examined. The respective goals of these chapters are to understand how Chinese American and Filipino American adolescents conceptualize the quality of parent-adolescent relationships and the negotiation of autonomy and parental control.

Our studies provide multiple approaches to the investigation of the measurement and meanings of the cultural foundations of parenting practices. Using both qualitative and quantitative methods, the studies employ comparisons between Asian American and European American adolescents and parents, as well as within-group analyses of differences and similarities between Chinese and Filipino American in measures of parenting and in understandings of parent-adolescent relationships and parenting practices.

References

Agbayani-Siewert, P. (1994). Filipino American culture and family: Guidelines for practitioners. *Families in Society*, *75*, 429–438.

Agbayani-Siewert, P., & Revilla, L. (1995). Filipino Americans. In P. G. Min (Ed.), *Asian Americans* (pp. 134–168). Thousand Oaks, CA: Sage.

Barber, B. K., & Harmon, E. L. (2002). Violating the self: Parental psychological control of children and adolescents. In B. K. Barber (Ed.), *Intrusive parenting: How psychological control affects children and adolescents* (pp. 15–52). Washington, DC: American Psychological Association.

Barber, B. K., Olsen, J. E., & Shagle, S. C. (1994). Associations between parental psychological and behavioral control and youth internalized and externalized behaviors. *Child Development*, *65*, 1120–1136.

Barber, B. K., Stolz, H. E., & Olsen. J. A. (2005). Parental support, psychological control, and behavioral control: Assessing relevance across time, culture, and method. *Monographs of the Society for Research in Child Development*, *70*, 1–137.

Barrera, M., Jr., Prelow, M., Dumka, L. E., Gonzales, N. A., Knight, G. P., Michaels, M. L., et al. (2002). Pathways from family economic conditions to adolescents' distress: Supportive parenting, stressors outside the family, and deviant peers. *Journal of Community Psychology*, *30*, 135–152.

Baumrind, D. (1967). Childcare practices anteceding three patterns of preschool behavior. *Genetic Psychology Monograph*, *75*(1), 43–88.

Baumrind, D. (1968). Authoritarian versus authoritative parental control. *Adolescence*, *3*, 255–272.

Baumrind, D. (1991). The influence of parenting style on adolescent competence and substance use. *Journal of Early Adolescence*, *11*, 56–95.

Berndt, T. J., Cheung, P. C., Lau, S., & Hau, K. (1993). Perceptions of parenting in mainland China, Taiwan, and Hong Kong: Sex differences and societal differences. *Developmental Psychology*, *29*, 156–164.

Blair, S. L., & Qian, Z. (1998). Family and Asian students' educational performance: A consideration of diversity. *Journal of Family Issues*, *19*, 355–374.

Bond, M., & Wang, S. (1983). Aggressive behaviour in Chinese society: The problem of maintaining order and harmony. *Bulletin of the Hong Kong Psychological Society*, *8*, 5–25.

Chao, R. K. (1994). Beyond parental control and authoritarian parenting style: Understanding Chinese parenting through the cultural notion of training. *Child Development*, *65*, 1111–1119.

Chao, R. K. (2001). Extending research on the consequences of parenting style for Chinese Americans and European Americans. *Child Development*, *72*, 1832–1843.

Chao, R. K., & Tseng, V. (2002). Parenting of Asians. In M. H. Bornstein (Ed.), *Handbook of parenting: Vol. 4. Social conditions and applied parenting* (2nd ed., pp. 59–93). Mahwah, NJ: Lawrence Erlbaum Associates Publishers.

Chen, X., Liu, M., & Li, D. (2000). Parental warmth, control, and indulgence and their relations to adjustment in Chinese children: A longitudinal study. *Journal of Family Psychology*, *14*, 401–419.

Chiu, L. (1987). Child-rearing attitudes of Chinese American, Chinese American–American, and European–American mothers. *International Journal of Psychology*, *22*, 409–419.

Collins, W. A., & Steinberg, L. (2006). Adolescent development in interpersonal context. In N. Eisenberg, W. Damon, & R. M. Lerner (Eds.), *Handbook of child psychology: Vol. 3. Social, emotional, and personality development* (6th ed., pp. 1003–1067). Hoboken, NJ: John Wiley & Sons Inc.

Conger, R. D., & Conger, K. J. (1993). Economic stress and early adjustment of adolescent girls. *Developmental Psychology, 29*, 206.

Conger, R. D., Conger, K. J., Elder, G. H., & Lorenz, F. O. (1992). A family process model of economic hardship and adjustment of early adolescent boys. *Child Development, 63*, 526–541.

Darling, N., & Steinberg, L. (1993). Parenting style as context: An integrative model. *Psychological Bulletin, 113*, 487–496.

Deater-Deckard, K., Dodge, K. A., Bates, J. E., & Pettit, G. S. (1996). Physical discipline among African American and European American mothers: Links to children's externalizing behaviors. *Developmental Psychology, 32*, 1065–1072.

Dornbusch, S. M. (1985). Single parents, extended households, and the control of adolescents. *Child Development, 56*, 326–341.

Dornbusch, S. M., Ritter, P. L., Leiderman, P. H., & Roberts, D. F. (1987). The relation of parenting style to adolescent school performance. *Child Development. Special Issue: Schools and development, 58*(5), 1244–1257.

Durbrow, E. H., Pena, L. F., Masten, A., Sesma, A., & Williamson, I. (2001). Mothers' conceptions of child competence in contexts of poverty: The Philippines, St. Vincent, and the United States. *International Journal of Behavioral Development, 25*, 438–443.

Fuligni, A. J. (1998). Authority, autonomy, and parent–adolescent conflict and cohesion: A study of adolescents from Mexican, Chinese, Filipino, and European backgrounds. *Developmental Psychology, 34*, 782–792.

Fuligni, A. J., & Pedersen, S. (2002). Family obligation and the transition to young adulthood. *Developmental Psychology, 38*, 856–868.

Fuligni, A. J., Yip, T., & Tseng, V. (2002). The impact of family obligation on the daily activities and psychological well-being of Chinese American adolescents. *Child Development, 73*, 302–314.

Fuligni, A. J., & Yoshikawa, H. (2002). Investments in children among immigrant families. In A. Kalil & T. DeLeire (Eds.), *Family investments in children's potential: Resources and parenting behavior that promote success*. Mahwah, NJ: Lawrence Erlbaum Associates Publishers.

Gallimore, R., Goldenberg, C. N., & Weisner, T. S. (1993). The social construction and subjective reality of activity settings: Implications for community psychology. *American Journal of Community Psychology, 21*, 537–559.

Ge, X. Best, K. M., Conger, R. D., & Simons, R. L. (1996). Parenting behaviors and the occurrence and co-occurrence of adolescent depressive symptoms and conduct problems. *Developmental Psychology, 32*, 717–731.

Gonzales, N. A., Cauce, A. M., & Mason, C. A. (1996). Inter-observer agreement in the assessment of parental behavior and parent–adolescent conflict: African American mothers, daughters, and independent observers. *Child Development, 67*, 1483–1498.

Goodnow, J. J., & Collins, W. A. (1990). *Development according to parents: The nature, sources and consequences of parents' ideas*. East Sussex: Laurence Erlbaum Associates Ltd.

Goodnow, J. J., & Grusec, J. E. (1994). Impact of parental discipline methods on the child's internalization of values. *Developmental Psychology, 30*, 4–19.

Greenberger, E.,& Chen, C. (1996). Perceived family relationships and depressed mood in early and late adolescence: A comparison of European and Asian Americans. *Developmental Psychology, 32*, 707–716.

Guthrie, P. J., & Jacobs, G. M. (1966) *Child rearing and personality development in the Philippines*. Pennsylvania, PA: Penn State University Press.

Hill, N. E. (2001). Parenting and academic socialization as they relate to school readiness: The roles of ethnicity and family income. *Journal of Educational Psychology, 93*, 686–697.

Huang, N. H. (1994). An integrative approach to clinical assessment and intervention with Asian–American Adolescents. *Journal of Clinical Child Psychology, 23*, 21–31.
Jacobson, K. C., & Crockett, L. J. (2000). Parental monitoring and adolescent adjustment: An ecological perspective. *Journal of Research on Adolescence, 10*, 65–97.
Julian, T. W., McHenry, P. C., & McKelvey, M. W. (1994). Cultural variations in parenting, perceptions of Caucasian, African American, Hispanic, and Asian American parents. *Family Relations, 43*, 30–37.
Knight, G. P., & Hill, N. E. (1998). Measurement equivalence in research involving minority adolescents. In V. McLoyd & L. Steinberg (Eds.), *Studying minority adolescents: Conceptual, methodological and theoretical issues* (pp. 183–210). Hillsdale, NJ: Lawrence Erlbaum Associates, Inc.
Knight, G. P., Virdin, L. M., Ocampo, K. A., & Roosa, M. (1994). An examination of the cross-ethnic equivalence of measures of negative life events and mental health among Hispanic and European American children. *American Journal of Community Psychology, 22*, 767–783.
Kornadt, H. J. (1987). The aggression motive and personality development: Japan and Germany. In F. Halish & J. Kuhl (Eds.), *Motivation, intention and volition*. Berlin: Springer-Verlag.
Kurdek, L. A., & Fine, M. A. (1994). Family acceptance and family control as predictors of adjustment in young adolescents: Linear, curvilinear, or interactive effects? *Child Development, 65*, 1137–1146.
Lamborn, S. D., Mounts, N. S., Steinberg, L., & Dornbusch, S. M. (1991). Patterns of competence and adjustment among adolescents from authoritative, authoritarian, indulgent, and neglectful families. *Child Development, 62*, 1049–1065.
Lansford, J. E., Chang, L., Dodge, K. A., Malone, P. S., Oburu, P., Palmerus, K., et al. (2005). Physical discipline and children's adjustment: Cultural normativeness as a moderator. *Child Development, 76*, 1129–1317.
Lansford, J. E., Deater-Deckard, K., Dodge, K. A., Bates, J. E., & Pettit, G. S. (2004). Ethnic differences in the link between physical discipline and later adolescent externalizing behaviors. *Journal of Child Psychology and Psychiatry, 45*, 801–812.
Lau, S., & Cheung, P. C. (1987). Relations between Chinese adolescents' perception of parental control and organization and their perception of parental warmth. *Developmental Psychology, 23*, 726–729.
Lau, S. Lew, W. J. F., Hau, K. T., Cheung, P. C., & Berndt, T. J. (1990). Relations among perceived parental control, warmth, indulgence, and family harmony of Chinese American in mainland China. *Developmental Psychology, 26*, 674–677.
Lin, C. C., & Fu, V. R. (1990). A comparison of child-rearing practices among Chinese American, immigrant Chinese American, and Caucasian-American parents. *Child Development, 61*(2), *Special Issue on Minority Children*, 429–433.
Maccoby, E. E., & Martin, J. A. (1983). Socialization in the context of the family: Parent–child interaction. In E. M. Hetherington (Ed.), *Handbook of child psychology: Vol. 4. Socialization, personality, and social development*. New York: Wiley.
Mason, C. A., Cauce, A. M., & Gonzales, N. (1997). Parents and peers in the lives of adolescents: An interactive approach to the study of human behavior. In R. W. Taylor & M. C. Wang (Eds.), *Social and emotional adjustment and family relations in ethnic minority families* (pp. 85–98). Mahwah, NJ: Lawrence Erlbaum Associates, Inc.
Min, P. G. (2006). *Asian Americans: Contemporary trends and issues*. Thousand Oaks, CA: Sage.
McLoyd, V. C. (1990). Minority children: Introduction to the special issue. *Child Development, 61*(2), 263.
Nomura, N., Noguchi, Y., Saito, S., & Tezuka, I. (1995). Family characteristics and dynamics in Japan and the United States: A preliminary report from the family environment scale. *International Journal of Intercultural Relations, 19*, 59–86.
Parke, R. D., & Buriel, R. (2006). Socialization in the family: Ethnic and ecological perspectives. In N. Eisenberg, W. Damon, & R. M. Lerner (Eds.), *Handbook of child psychology: Vol. 3. Social, emotional, and personality development* (6th ed., pp. 429–504). Hoboken, NJ: John Wiley & Sons Inc.

Pe-Pua, R., & Protacio-Marcelino, E. (2000). Sikolohiyang Pilipino (Filipino psychology): A legacy of Virgilio G. Enriquez. *Asian Journal of Social Psychology*, *3*, 49–71.

Pinderhughes, E. E., Dodge, K. A., Bates, J. E., Pettit, G. S., & Zelli, A. (2000). Discipline responses: Influences of parents' socioeconomic status, ethnicity, beliefs about parenting, stress, and cognitive-emotional processes. *Journal of Family Psychology*, *14*, 380–400.

Pinderhughes, E. E., Nix, R., Foster, E. M., & Jones, D. (2001). Parenting in context: Impact of neighborhood poverty, residential stability, public services, social networks, and danger on parental behaviors. *Journal of Marriage and Family*, *63*, 941–953.

Rhee, S., Chang, J., & Rhee, J. (2003). Acculturation, communication patterns, and self-esteem among Asian and Caucasian American adolescents. *Adolescence*, *38*, 749–768.

Rohner, R. P. (1986). *The warmth dimension: Foundations of parental acceptance-rejection theory*. Thousand Oaks, CA: Sage Publications.

Rohner, R. P., & Pettengill, S. M. (1985). Perceived parental acceptance-rejection and parental control among Korean adolescents. *Child Development*, *56*, 524–528.

Shumow, L., & Lomax, R. (2002). Parental efficacy: Predictor of parenting behavior and adolescent outcomes. *Parenting: Science & Practice*, *2*, 127.

Steinberg, L., Elmen, J. D., & Mounts, N. S. (1989). Authoritative parenting, psychosocial maturity, and academic success among adolescents. *Child Development*, *60*, 1424–1436.

Steinberg, L., Lamborn, S. D., Darling, N., & Mounts, N. S. (1994). Over-time changes in adjustment and competence among adolescents from authoritative, authoritarian, indulgent, and neglectful families. *Child Development*, *65*, 754–770.

Steinberg, L., Mounts, N., Lamborn, S., & Dornbusch, S. (1991). Authoritative parenting and adolescent adjustment across varied ecological niches. *Journal of Research on Adolescence*, *1*, 19–36.

Stice, E., & Barrera, M., Jr. (1995). A longitudinal examination of the reciprocal relations between perceived parenting and adolescents' substance use and externalizing behaviors. *Developmental Psychology*, *31*, 322–334.

Taylor, R. D., Casten, R., & Flickinger, S. M. (1993). Influence of kinship social support on the parenting experiences and psychosocial adjustment of African American adolescents. *Developmental Psychology*, *29*, 382–388.

Taylor, R. D., & Roberts, D. (1995). Kinship support and maternal and adolescent well-being in economically disadvantaged African-American families. *Child Development*, *66*, 1585–1597.

Trommsdorff, G. (1985). Some comparative aspects of socialization in Japan and Germany. In I. R. Lagunes & Y. H. Poortinga (Eds.), *From a different perspective: Studies of behavior across cultures* (pp. 231–240). Lisse: Swets & Zeitlinger.

Uba, L. (1994). *Asian Americans: Personality patterns, identity, and mental health*. New York, NY: Guilford Press.

Wu, S. (2001). Parenting in Chinese American families. In N. B. Webb (Ed.), *Culturally diverse parent–child and family relationships: A guide for social workers and other practitioners* (pp. 235–260). New York: Columbia University Press Publishers.

Wu, C. X., & Chao, R. K. (2005). Intergenerational cultural conflicts for Chinese American youth with immigrant parents: Norms of parental warmth and the consequences. *International Journal of Behavioral Development*, *29*, 516–523.

Chapter 2
Do Measures of Parenting Have the Same Meaning for European, Chinese, and Filipino American Adolescents? Tests of Measurement Equivalence

Lisa J. Crockett, Glen J. Veed, and Stephen T. Russell

As outlined in Chapter 1, intriguing differences between European Americans and Asian Americans have emerged in earlier studies of parenting. According to these studies, Asian American parents are more restrictive and control-oriented and express less overt warmth than European American parents (Bond & Wang, 1983; Chiu, 1987; Lin & Fu, 1990; Wu & Chao, 2005). However, most of the work to date has focused on Chinese American samples and less is known about other Asian groups, such as Filipino Americans, although recent studies have begun to fill this gap (Agbayani-Siewert, 1994; Fuligni & Pedersen, 2002; Pe-Pua & Protacio-Marcelino, 2000).

There is reason to suspect that the meaning of some parenting practices differs cross-ethnically owing to distinct parenting philosophies and cultural norms (Chao, 1994; Lansford et al., 2005). For example, the meaning of control behaviors may vary among Chinese-, Filipino-, and European Americans: they may be viewed more positively by Asian American cultural groups, especially Chinese Americans (Lau, Lew, Hau, Cheung, & Berndt, 1990; Nomura, Noguchi, Saito, & Tezuka, 1995). Thus, Chinese and Filipino adolescents may be more likely to interpret parental control behaviors as a form of caring and to accept these behaviors as legitimate (Fuligni, 1998; Lam, 2003). Furthermore, the behaviors that signal parental support may differ across cultural groups, with direct expressions of warmth and affection being more central to European Americans' than to Asian Americans' conceptions of support (Chao, 2001a; Wu & Chao, 2005). If so, direct expressions of warmth might be less relevant to Asian American teenagers' perceptions of being loved and supported. The differing interpretations of parental control and support raise the possibility that Asian Americans and European Americans hold distinct notions of parenting. Furthermore, Chinese American and Filipino American adolescents might differ from each other in their understanding of parental support and control. Filipino Americans are less likely than Chinese Americans to emphasize traditional Asian cultural values perhaps

---

L.J. Crockett (✉)
University of Nebraska, Lincoln, NE, USA
e-mail: ecrockett1@unl.edu

S.T. Russell et al. (eds.), *Asian American Parenting and Parent-Adolescent Relationships*, Advancing Responsible Adolescent Development,
DOI 10.1007/978-1-4419-5728-3_2,

owing to the extended history of Spanish and US influence in the Philippines and the influence of Catholicism. Such differences could lead to subtle or not so subtle differences in socialization goals, parenting norms, and children's interpretation of parental behaviors.

Cultural perspectives on parenting support the notion of cultural differences in the meaning of parenting behaviors. Value orientations and associated "cultural scripts" inform parenting practices and parent-child relationships, as well as family members' understandings of their relationships (Greenfield, 1994). More broadly, parenting practices reflect parents' ethnotheories (or cultural beliefs about parenting and child development; Super & Harkness, 1986) and cultural notions of desirable human characteristics. Presumably these ethnotheories and values are transmitted to children in the course of socialization. Thus, cultural values and scripts constitute an important frame of reference for children's expectations regarding parent-child relationships and interpretations of parents' behavior.

Such differences in conceptions of parenting pose challenges for measuring parenting behaviors across different ethnic groups. If parental support (or control) encompasses different behaviors among European Americans than Chinese Americans, a scale designed to measure that construct in one group is likely to omit behaviors that are important for defining it in the other group, resulting in different levels of the validity of that measure for the two cultural groups. Moreover, even if the same items (behaviors) are relevant in both groups, they may be interpreted somewhat differently or may be more central to one group's understanding of the construct than the other's. Such differences can result in differential measure validity and distinct measurement properties in the two groups. It follows that use of such a measure in cross-cultural or cross-ethnic work could lead to inaccurate inferences about group differences in parental support or its effects. For this reason, measures that have been developed primarily from the perspective of one cultural or ethnic group need to be examined and validated in other groups before cross-cultural comparisons are made. Most measures of parenting have been developed primarily with European American samples (Julian, McHenry, & McKelvey, 1994), and the question of measurement equivalence for Asian populations—or the degree to which a measure of parenting has the same meaning or is "equivalent" across groups—has rarely been addressed. Unless measurement equivalence is established, it is difficult to determine whether ethnic differences in scores reflect true differences in parenting or differences in the meaning of the parenting measures.

From another perspective, an examination of measurement equivalence can provide information on cross-cultural similarities and differences in conceptions of parenting. A lack of equivalence in measures may indicate differences between groups in the meaning or importance of particular parenting behaviors. For example, a measure of autonomy granting (i.e., low levels of parental control) that exhibits a different factor structure among Filipino Americans and Chinese Americans may indicate different clusters of parenting behaviors or dimensions of parental control experienced in each group. Thus, finding measurement equivalence increases confidence in a parenting measure but also provides evidence supporting cross-cultural similarities in the parenting constructs under study. Conversely, a failure to find measurement equivalence makes cross-cultural comparisons suspect and may also point to cultural differences in the interpretation or salience of particular parenting behaviors.

In this chapter, we investigate the cross-ethnic equivalence of parenting measures using data from the National Longitudinal Study of Adolescent Health (Add Health Study). The "Add Health" Study was begun in the mid-1990s and is the largest, most comprehensive study of adolescents in the United States. The study is unique because it includes a range of measures about parenting and parent-adolescent relationships. In addition, the original in-home survey involved over 20,000 US adolescents, and included a specific over-sample of Chinese American adolescents. Thus, the study allows us to examine adolescents' reports of their relationships with their parents and their parents' parenting behaviors for over 8,550 European American, 250 Chinese American, and over 450 Filipino American adolescents. Our analyses were designed with two goals in mind: first, to learn whether the measures of parental support and control (framed as autonomy granting) show measurement equivalence/invariance and, second, to gain insight into the different understandings of parental support and autonomy granting held by Chinese American, Filipino American, and European American adolescents.

How Similar Are Measures Across Ethnic Groups?

Lack of measurement equivalence can occur for several reasons (Hui & Triandis, 1985; Knight & Hill, 1998). At the most basic level, there may be a lack of construct equivalence, such that each group conceptualizes parental support differently (Crockett, Randall, Shen, Russell, & Driscoll, 2005; Hui & Triandis, 1985). If so, a measure of parental support developed for one group (e.g., European Americans) would fail to capture relevant aspects of support as understood by the other group (e.g., Filipino Americans). Even if the construct is the same in both groups, the measure utilized could assess that construct more poorly in one group than the other, making scores for that group less accurate. Finally, for a given measure, different groups may interpret the possible response options differently or utilize a different metric when answering, resulting in a lack of scalar equivalence (Hui & Triandis, 1985). In such cases, a particular score would reflect different *amounts* of the construct in the two groups (e.g., an identical score might indicate high parental support in one group but only moderate parental support in another). For example, if Asian Americans are less likely than European Americans to endorse positively worded questions (Bae & Brekke, 2003), we would expect to see ethnic differences in perceived parenting even if actual levels of parenting behaviors are the same. The problem of measurement nonequivalence also extends to heterogeneity within racial or ethnic groups, in this case Asian Americans. Chinese Americans and Filipino Americans represent distinct nationalities, historical influences, and cultural traditions, which may influence each group's normative patterns of parenting, their understandings of parental support and autonomy granting, and their responses to parenting measures.

Studies of measurement equivalence typically include an assessment of factorial invariance across groups (Vandenberg & Lance, 2000), that is, whether the scale that is used by respondents is comparable across groups. The assessment of factorial invariance is based on multi-group confirmatory factor analysis (CFA). A series of models is tested in which progressively stricter constraints are added, reflecting increasingly stringent levels of cross-group invariance. First, configural invariance is examined to see whether a set of items are related in similar ways across groups: do the same items form a cluster or factor in each ethnic group? If configural invariance is supported, weak (metric) invariance is examined (equality of factor loadings across groups): do the items have the same relative contribution to the measure across groups? If weak or metric invariance can be established, the next step is to test for strong (scalar) invariance (equality of item intercepts as well as factor loading across groups): are the average scores on each item in the measure equal across groups? Finally, if metric and scalar invariance can be established, the final step is to test for strict invariance (equality of unique item error variances as well as factor loadings and intercepts across groups): if the loading and average score for each item are the same for each group, is the error variance the same across groups as well? The fit of the model after each new constraint is added is compared to that of the preceding model using a chi-square difference test: significant increases in χ^2 indicate a decrement in model fit and a lack of invariance. Partial invariance is also possible at each stage, where some but not all items are invariant across groups (Byrne, Shavelson, & Muthén, 1989; Vandenberg & Lance, 2000).

We examined the factorial invariance of Add Health measures of parental support and autonomy granting in order to assess the equivalence of these measures for European American, Chinese American, and Filipino American boys and girls and, further, to explore whether adolescents in these three ethnic groups have similar understandings of parental support and autonomy. Analyses were conducted separately for girls and boys, and separate measures of maternal and paternal support were included because other research indicates that children's perceptions of their relationships with parents depend on both the gender of the adolescent and the gender of the parent (Berndt, Cheung, Lau, & Hau, 1993; Crockett, Brown, Russell, & Shen, 2007; Crockett, Brown, Iturbide, Russell, & Wilkinson-Lee, 2009; Youniss & Smollar, 1985).

Method

Sample

The National Longitudinal Study of Adolescent Health (Add Health) was designed to examine the health status of adolescents, as well as influences on their health-related behaviors. The study includes a nationally representative sample of US adolescents in grades 7–12 based on a multistage, stratified, school-based, cluster sampling design. Specifically, a sample of 80 high schools and 52 middle schools from the United States (132 schools) was selected to be representative of US schools with respect to region of country, urbanicity, school type, ethnicity, and school size (Udry, 1998). The students in those schools were invited to participate.

Students who completed an in-school questionnaire or who were listed on a school roster of one of the participating schools were eligible to complete an In-Home Interview. A representative sample of these youth (the core sample) was selected and supplemented with several subsamples. Some ethnic groups were sampled in proportion to their size within the US population, whereas others (e.g., Chinese Americans, Cuban Americans, Puerto Ricans) were oversampled to ensure adequate sample sizes for analysis (Bearman, Jones, & Udry, 1997). The survey was conducted in English; thus non-English-speaking Asian American adolescents would be under-represented in our analyses.

The sample for the present analysis was based on over 20,000 adolescents who completed the first In-Home Interview (Wave 1; contractual data set). To be included in the present analysis, adolescents had to be between the ages of 12 and 18 at Wave 1, have valid sample weights, and self-identify as non-Hispanic White (European American), Chinese, or Filipino. If more than one adolescent in a family participated, one sibling was randomly selected for inclusion in order to eliminate potential dependency in the data. The final analytic sample included 9,262 youth (51% female): 8,550 European Americans, 253 Chinese Americans, and 459 Filipino Americans. The sample size for analyses of paternal support was substantially smaller than for other parenting variables because data on paternal support was obtained only from adolescents with a resident father. Otherwise, the amount of missing data was trivial, resulting in the loss of no more than 12 cases for any particular subgroup in the analysis.

Measures

Race/ethnicity. Respondents were classified into racial/ethnic groups based on their responses to four questions. Race was based on two questions: (1) "What is your race?" and (2) "Which one category best describes your racial background?" (For each question, the response options were: White, Black or African American, American Indian or Native American, Asian or Pacific Islander). Ethnicity was based on a third question, "Are you of Hispanic or Latino origin?" (*no, yes*). Finally, Asian adolescents were asked, "What is your Asian background?" Non-Latinos were selected for the present analysis. They were classified as European American if they endorsed "White" as their only race or as the category that "best" described their racial background; they were classified respectively as Chinese American or Filipino American if they selected Asian as their only or best racial background and then selected Chinese American (Filipino American) as their Asian origin.

Perceived maternal and paternal support. For each resident parent, adolescents responded to five items indexing the level of parental warmth and caring:

1. How close to you feel to your mother [father]?
2. How much do you think she [he] cares about you?

3. Most of the time, your mother [father] is warm and loving to you.
4. You are satisfied with the way your mother [father] and you communicate with each other.
5. Overall, you are satisfied with your relationship with your mother [father].

For the first two questions, response options ranged from 1 (*not at all*) to 5 (*very much*); for the remaining questions, responses ranged from 1 (*strongly disagree*) to 5 (*strongly agree*). Because support from non-resident fathers was not assessed in the Add Health survey, only adolescents with resident fathers were included in analyses of paternal support.

Perceived parental autonomy granting. Parental autonomy granting was assessed by asking adolescents whether their parents allowed them to make their own decisions in six areas. Possible responses were 0 (*no*) or 1 (*yes*). Specifically, adolescents were asked, "Do your parents let you make your own decisions about":

1. the people you hang around with?
2. what you wear?
3. how much television you watch?
4. which television programs you watch?
5. what time you go to bed on weeknights?
6. what you eat?

Analytic Approach

We examined the factorial invariance of the three parenting measures (maternal support, paternal support, and autonomy granting) using confirmatory factor analysis (CFA) in MPlus. A series of CFAs was conducted separately by gender to examine configural, weak, strong, and strict factorial invariance. First, to investigate configural invariance, we tested the fit of a one-factor solution of each parenting measure separately for European Americans, Chinese Americans, and Filipino Americans of each gender. If the model showed adequate fit in two ethnic groups (e.g., European American and Filipino American boys), cross-ethnic configural invariance was supported for those groups.

If configural invariance between two ethnic groups was supported, we used multigroup CFA to examine weak, strong, and strict factorial invariance across those two groups. Following recommendations outlined by Vandenberg and Lance (2000), a series of two-group models was tested to examine the effect of constraining specific parameters to be equal across groups. In the first (unconstrained) model, factor loadings, item intercepts, and item error variances were allowed to vary across groups (Model 1). In the second model (weak invariance), corresponding factor loadings were constrained to be equal across the two groups (Model 2). If weak invariance was supported, we proceeded to examine strong invariance by constraining corresponding item intercepts as well as factor loadings to be equal across groups (Model 3). Finally, if strong invariance was supported, we examined strict invariance by further constraining corresponding item error variances to be equal across groups (Model 4).

To assess model fit, we used the Satorra-Bentler scaled chi square, which is based on a maximum likelihood estimator with robust standard errors (MRL in MPlus; also known as the Yuan-Bentler T2 statistic [Yuan & Bentler, 2000]). Because the chi-square test is sensitive to sample size (Kline, 1998), we also examined other fit indices including the Comparative Fit Index (CFI), the Root Mean Squared Error of Approximation (RMSEA), and the Standardized Root Mean Square Residual (SRMR). Adequate fit was indicated by a CFI greater than 0.90 and RMSEA and SRMR less than 0.10 (Jöreskog & Sörbom, 1998; Kelloway, 1998; Kline, 1998; Maruyama, 1998). A chi-square difference test, calculated as recommended by Muthén and Muthén (1998–2007), was used to compare the fit of successive models (e.g., Model 1 and Model 2). A significant increase in the chi-square value indicates a decrement in model fit, and this change in fit was the basis for assessing factorial invariance. For example, if constraining corresponding factor loadings to be equal across groups did not result in a significant increase in the chi-square value when compared to the unconstrained model, weak factorial invariance was supported. However, if the chi-square value was significantly larger once corresponding factor loadings were constrained to be equal across groups, the significant decrement in model fit indicated that weak invariance was not supported. If invariance was not supported at any stage, tests of partial metric invariance were conducted to see whether a subset of items was invariant (Byrne et al., 1989; Kline, 1998; Vandenberg & Lance, 2000).

In the Add Health study, schools were sampled and adolescents in those schools recruited. Because adolescents from the same school are more similar to each other than they are to adolescents from other schools, the sample is subject to a clustering effect. In addition, certain groups of adolescents were oversampled to ensure adequate sample sizes for analysis. Sample weights are applied to ensure that the sample represents the national population. Failure to take these aspects of the sampling design into account will lead to inaccurate point estimates and standard errors, biasing results toward finding differences between groups (Chantala & Tabor, 1999). To avoid this problem, CFAs were conducted in Mplus, which can adjust for both sample weights and clustering effects (Muthén & Muthén, 1998–2007). All CFAs included sample weights and accounted for the clustered design. In contrast, descriptive statistics were estimated using SAS; these analyses included sample weights but did not adjust for the clustering effect.

Results

Demographic characteristics of the analytic sample based on weighted data are provided in Table 2.1 (these descriptive analyses were conducted in SAS and did not adjust for the complex sample design). The ethnic subsamples included roughly equal numbers of boys and girls. On average, parent education differed significantly across ethnic groups. Filipino girls reported higher levels of maternal education and

Table 2.1 Means (standard errors) or percentages for demographic variables, parental support, and autonomy measures by ethnic group and gender

	European American		Filipino American		Chinese American	
	Boys ($N = 4{,}132$)	Girls ($N = 4{,}418$)	Boys ($N = 234$)	Girls ($N = 225$)	Boys ($N = 135$)	Girls ($N = 118$)
Age	15.38 (0.03)^{a}	15.27 (0.03)^{a}	15.59 (0.11)	15.83 (0.12)	15.57 (0.14)	15.24 (0.16)
Maternal education	5.58 (0.04)^{a}	5.55 (0.03)^{b}	5.91 (0.18)	6.45 (0.17)^{a,b}	5.21 (0.24)	6.58 (0.26)
Paternal education	5.74 (0.04)^{a}	5.73 (0.04)^{b}	6.15 (0.17)	6.36 (0.17)	5.45 (0.28)	7.23 (0.25)^{a,b}
Financial problems	12%	13%	9%	14%	9%	1%
Maternal support	4.49 (0.01)^{a,b,c}	4.38 (0.01)^{a}	4.50 (0.04)^{d}	4.20 (0.05)^{c,d}	4.15 (0.04)^{b}	4.40 (0.05)
Paternal support	4.31 (0.01)^{a,b,c}	4.22 (0.01)^{a}	4.32 (0.05)	4.02 (0.06)^{c}	3.91 (0.08)^{b}	4.32 (0.07)
Autonomy	4.97 (0.02)^{a}	5.13 (0.02)^{a,b}	4.72 (0.12)	4.47 (0.13)^{b}	4.69 (0.14)	4.85 (0.16)

Note: Maximum N is listed; N's varied across measures due to missing values. Means with the same superscripts are significantly different from each other (Tukey). Parents reported their educational level and financial problems (difficulty paying bills).

Chinese girls reported higher levels of paternal education than European American girls and boys. Regarding the parenting variables, European American boys reported higher levels of maternal and paternal support than Chinese American boys. Additionally, European American girls reported higher levels of autonomy granting than Filipino American girls. These differences should be viewed with caution unless measurement equivalence is established. Gender differences within ethnic group also were found: among European Americans, boys were slightly older and reported higher levels of maternal and paternal support than girls; among Filipino Americans, boys reported higher levels of maternal support than did girls.

Maternal Support

To examine configural invariance, a one-factor solution for the five maternal support items was tested separately for boys and girls in each ethnic group. Error terms of items that were adjacent to each other in the interview questionnaire were allowed to correlate to improve model fit. As shown in Table 2.2, the one-factor solution for maternal support fit well for European American girls and boys as indicated by CFIs of 0.98 and RMSEAs and SRMRs of 0.06 or less. (A correlated error term for satisfaction with communication and satisfaction with overall relationship was added for boys, and a correlated error term for perceived closeness to mother and perceived maternal caring was added for girls.) The one-factor model also fit well for Filipino American boys and girls after adding the same correlated error term as for European American boys: CFIs were 0.97 or higher; RMSEA and SRMR were 0.06 or lower. However, the model did not fit well for Chinese Americans of either gender. For boys, the fit indices suggested good fit, but three of the five items

Table 2.2 Fit indices for measures of maternal support, paternal support, and autonomy granting for males and females in three ethnic groups

	N	X^2	CFI	RMSEA	SRMR
Maternal support					
European American					
Boys	3,846	58.08**[,a]	0.98	0.06	0.03
Girls	4,152	52.37**[,a]	0.98	0.05	0.03
Chinese American					
Boys	134	2.57[a]	1.00	0.01	0.05
Girls	113	27.32**	0.74	0.20	0.06
Filipino American					
Boys	216	7.37[a]	0.97	0.06	0.02
Girls	210	4.40[a]	1.00	0.02	0.04
Paternal support					
European American					
Boys	3,304	80.01**[,b]	0.97	0.09	0.02
Girls	3,344	52.82**[,b]	0.98	0.07	0.02
Chinese American					
Boys	123	217.04**	0.50	0.59	0.07
Girls	105	6.37	0.99	0.05	0.02
Filipino American					
Boys	189	5.12[a]	0.99	0.04	0.03
Girls	184	7.94*[,b]	0.98	0.10	0.03
Autonomy granting[c]					
European American					
Boys	4,069	64.47**	0.96	0.04	
Girls	4,298	123.36**	0.95	0.05	
Chinese American					
Boys	134	8.00	1.00	0.01	
Girls	116	22.94**	0.88	0.12	
Filipino American					
Boys	228	13.18	0.96	0.05	
Girls	222	12.71	0.97	0.04	

* $p < 0.05$
** $p < 0.01$
[a] 1 pair of correlated errors.
[b] 2 pairs of correlated errors.
[c] Based on categorical CFA; SRMR is not available.

(perceived closeness to mother, perceived maternal caring, and perceived maternal warmth) failed to load significantly on the maternal support factor. For Chinese girls, the model fit was poor, as reflected in a low CFI and a high RMSEA value.

Because evidence of configural invariance was supported for European Americans and Filipino Americans, we proceeded to examine additional aspects of factorial invariance of the maternal support measure in those two ethnic groups using multiple group CFAs. To assess weak invariance, the fit of a two-group model in which corresponding factor loadings were constrained to be equal across the two ethnic groups was compared to that of an unconstrained model in which factor loadings were allowed to vary across groups. Model fit statistics appear in Table 2.3; unconstrained factor loadings are reported in Table 2.4.

Table 2.3 Two-group (European and Filipino American) metric invariance for parental support and autonomy for males and females

	X^2 (df)	CFI	RMSEA	SRMR	X^2 Difference (df)
Maternal support					
Boys ($N = 3,462$)					
Model 1: Unconstrained	81.00 (8)	0.97	0.07	0.03	
Model 2: Weak invariance	76.13 (12)	0.97	0.05	0.05	6.04 (4)
Model 3: Strong invariance	90.29 (16)	0.97	0.05	0.05	6.13 (4)
Model 4: Strict invariance	84.49 (21)	0.98	0.04	0.13	9.35 (5)
Girls ($N = 3,676$)					
Model 1: Unconstrained	60.68 (8)	0.98	0.06	0.03	
Model 2: Weak invariance	63.75 (12)	0.98	0.04	0.03	0.90 (4)
Model 3: Strong invariance	72.21 (16)	0.98	0.04	0.03	5.12 (4)
Model 4: Strict invariance	74.22 (21)	0.98	0.03	0.14	11.73* (5)
Paternal support					
Boys ($N = 2,804$)					
Model 1: Unconstrained	69.04 (6)	0.98	0.08	0.02	
Model 2: Weak invariance	90.22 (10)	0.97	0.07	0.09	16.53** (4)
Girls ($N = 3,676$)					
Model 1: Unconstrained	61.57 (6)	0.98	0.07	0.02	
Model 2: Weak invariance	55.25 (10)	0.99	0.05	0.04	5.77 (4)
Model 3: Strong invariance	61.46 (14)	0.99	0.04	0.04	1.17 (4)
Model 4: Strict invariance	56.08 (19)	0.99	0.03	0.04	1.11 (5)
Autonomy granting[a]					
Boys ($N = 3,462$)					
Model 1: Unconstrained	67.23 (18)	0.97	0.04		
Model 2: Weak invariance	118.78 (29)	0.94	0.04		52.21 (11)***

*$p<0.05$, **$p<0.01$,*** $p<0.001$
[a]Based on categorical CFA; SRMR is not available.

For European American and Filipino American boys, a chi-square difference test revealed that factor loadings for all of the maternal support items could be constrained to be equal across ethnic groups without significantly reducing model fit, supporting weak invariance (see Table 2.3). Next, we constrained the item intercepts (as well as factor loadings) for corresponding items to be equal across groups (Model 3) and compared the model fit to that of the preceding model (Model 2). These additional constraints did not result in a significant increase in chi square, so strong invariance was also supported. Finally, item error variances were constrained to be equal across groups as well. These additional constraints did not result in a significant increase in chi square, and the CFI and RMSEA indicated good model fit, supporting strict invariance. However, the SRMR was 0.13, suggesting poor model fit. Thus the support for strict invariance of the maternal support measure was qualified.

Among European American and Filipino American girls, constraining corresponding factor loadings of the maternal support items to be equal across

Table 2.4 Standardized factor loadings of parental support for males and females in two ethnic groups

	Boys		Girls	
Items	European American	Filipino American	European American	Filipino American
Maternal support				
How close to mother	0.52	0.69	0.59	0.63
How much she cares about you	0.24	0.25	0.23	0.22
Mother is warm and loving	0.47	0.44	0.59	0.62
Satisfied with communication	0.59	0.66	0.93	0.96
Satisfied with relationship	0.57	0.51	0.87	0.84
Paternal support				
How close to father	0.66	0.46	0.79	0.93
How much he cares about you	0.36[a]	0.16[a]	0.38	0.43
Father is warm and loving	0.75	0.79	0.78	1.00
Satisfied with communication	0.76[a]	0.88[a]	0.85	0.79
Satisfied with relationship	0.75	0.71	0.85	0.80

[a]Factor loadings could not be constrained to be equal between groups.

groups (Model 2) did not reduce model fit, supporting weak factorial invariance. Constraining item intercepts to be equal (Model 3) also failed to reduce model fit, so strong invariance was supported. However, constraining error variances to be equal across groups (Model 4) resulted in a significant increase in chi square as well as a high SRMR (0.14), indicating poor model fit. Thus strict invariance was not supported for girls. We examined partial strict invariance by systematically freeing error variances and comparing the fit of the partially constrained model with that of the strong invariance model (Model 3). Once the item on perceived closeness to mother was freed, the chi-square difference test was not significant. Thus, four of the five items showed strict invariance. In summary, results revealed evidence of configural, weak, and strong factorial invariance of the maternal support measure for European American and Filipino adolescents of both genders as well as qualified evidence of strict invariance. In contrast, for Chinese American adolescents, the maternal support measure failed to meet the fundamental requirement of configural invariance.

Paternal Support

Configural invariance for paternal support was examined in a similar manner, by testing a one-factor solution separately for boys and girls in each ethnic group. As shown in Table 2.2, the one-factor solution fit adequately for European American girls and boys (two correlated error terms, one for satisfaction with communication and satisfaction with overall relationship and one for closeness to father and perceived paternal caring, were added for each gender). The one-factor solution also fit adequately for Filipino American boys and girls (the same correlated error terms used for European Americans were added for Filipinas, whereas only the correlated error term for closeness to father and perceived paternal caring was added for Filipino American boys). For Filipino American girls, the CFI and SRMR indicated acceptable fit, but the RMSEA value approached the cut-off value of 0.10 suggesting marginal fit. In contrast, the one-factor model did not fit well for Chinese Americans of either gender. For Chinese American boys, the fit indices indicated very poor fit (low CFI; high RMSEA). For Chinese American girls, the fit indices appeared good but one of the five items, ("How much do you think your father cares about you?") failed to load significantly on the paternal support factor. Taken together, these results support configural invariance of the paternal support measure for European American and Filipino American adolescents but not for Chinese youth.

Based on these results we proceeded to examine more stringent types of factorial invariance among Filipino and European American adolescents. For boys, two-group CFAs showed that constraining factor loadings to be equal across groups resulted in a significant increase in chi square, so weak invariance was not supported (see Table 2.3 for fit statistics). Tests of partial weak invariance indicated that factor loadings of three paternal support items could be constrained to be equal across groups without a significant increase in the chi-square value (i.e., they were invariant); however, constraining the loadings for the remaining two items ("How much do you think he cares about you?" and "You are satisfied with the way your father and you communicate with each other") resulted in a significant decrement in model fit. As shown in Table 2.4, the factor loading for caring was higher for European American boys, whereas the loading for communication was higher for Filipino Americans. Because these items were not invariant only partial weak invariance was supported for European and Filipino American boys. In contrast, for Filipino American and European American girls, factor loadings, intercepts, and item error variances could each be constrained to be equal across groups without significantly reducing model fit. Thus, weak, strong, and strict factorial invariance were all supported (see Table 2.3).

Autonomy Granting

A one-factor solution was also examined to assess configural invariance in the measure of autonomy granting. In this case, we used a categorical CFA, because the items were dichotomous. The one-factor model showed an adequate fit for European American boys and girls and for Filipino American boys (see Table 2.2); however, in the other three groups one or more items failed to load significantly on the autonomy factor. (For Filipino American girls, the factor loading for the item on deciding what to eat was not significant. For Chinese American girls, loadings for the items regarding what to wear and what to eat were not significant, and for Chinese American boys, loadings for items on how much television to watch and when to go to bed on week nights were not significant.) Accordingly, further tests of factorial invariance were restricted to Filipino American and European American boys.

We could not assess weak invariance for the autonomy-granting measure because in categorical CFA the factor loadings and thresholds need to be constrained simultaneously. Therefore, we examined strong invariance for Filipino American and European American boys. The fit of a model in which factor loadings and thresholds were constrained to be equal across groups was compared to that of an unconstrained model in which factor loadings, item intercepts, and error variances were allowed to vary. In this case, the chi-square difference test was significant, so strong invariance was not supported (see Table 2.3). We examined partial strong invariance; however, results indicated that none of the items was invariant across groups.

In summary, results afforded strong evidence of cross-ethnic equivalence of the maternal support measure between European American and Filipino American adolescents of both genders in that configural, metric invariance, and strong invariance were supported for both boys and girls. Results regarding strict invariance were more equivocal, but partial strict invariance was found for girls and mixed evidence was found for boys. Concerning the measure of paternal support, there was evidence of strict factorial invariance between European American and Filipino American adolescent girls, but only partial weak invariance was supported for boys. For autonomy granting, there was evidence of configural invariance between European American and Filipino American boys but not between European American and Filipino American girls. There was no evidence of factorial invariance between Chinese Americans and either of the other groups on any of the parenting measures, as the basic test of configural invariance failed in each case.

Discussion

The goal of this chapter was to investigate the cross-ethnic equivalence of measures of parental support and autonomy granting across representative samples of European American, Chinese American, and Filipino American adolescents in order to elucidate possible cross-cultural similarities and differences in the meaning of these measures. To this end, we examined factorial invariance across ethnic groups separately by gender. The picture that emerged is one of considerable cross-ethnic invariance of the Add Health measures of maternal and paternal support for European Americans and Filipino Americans of both genders but not for Chinese Americans. In contrast, the evidence of cross-ethnic equivalence of the autonomy-granting measure was generally weak, suggesting that this measure may have different meanings for Asian American and European American adolescents.

Results for Filipino Americans and European Americans indicated that these two groups have similar understandings of maternal and paternal support. For both of these measures, configural invariance and either full or partial weak invariance was supported for both genders. Configural invariance suggests that two groups share a common frame of reference for the construct under study (Ghorpade, Hattrup, & Lackritz, 1999). Thus, Filipino and European Americans appear to conceptualize or perceive parental support in similar ways, at least with respect to the items included in the Add Health measures. The similarity in factor structure also indicates that the dimensions of maternal or paternal support tapped by the items are similar in both ethnic groups. Additionally, the support for strong invariance of the maternal support measure for European Americans and Filipino Americans of both genders indicates that the items are weighted similarly by members of both groups in defining the underlying dimension of maternal support and that both groups use the same metric in responding to the items. Furthermore, the evidence of strong invariance indicates that scores on the latent variable underlying this measure are comparable for Filipino and European Americans, although documentation of strict invariance would be desirable before raw scores are compared.

For paternal support the evidence of strict invariance between European and Filipino American girls indicates that scale scores for these two groups have the same meaning and can be compared. In contrast, the results for boys suggest the need for greater caution in making cross-group comparisons. In particular, two paternal support items regarding caring and satisfaction with communication were not invariant and loaded more strongly for one group of boys than the other. Caring loaded more strongly for European American boys, which suggests that it is more central to their notions of paternal support; however, satisfaction with communication loaded more strongly for Filipino American boys. Prior research on Asian parents indicates that they are less likely than European American parents to express warmth (Chao, 2001a; Wu & Chao, 2005), so we might expect a weaker loading for caring among Filipinos (as was found). However it is unclear why satisfaction with communication would be a stronger indicator for Filipino boys. Most prior research has focused on Chinese Americans, and Filipino American parents may be different (e.g., more accepting of open communication). Additional studies of this measure in Filipino samples are needed to replicate our results and to further probe the reasons that satisfaction with communication appears more central to Filipino American boys' notions of paternal support. Interestingly, *t* tests indicated no significant ethnic differences in reported levels of either maternal or paternal support for either gender. Thus, it appears that Filipino and European American adolescents of the same gender perceive similar levels of parental support.

The picture that emerged for autonomy granting was quite different. Configural invariance was found only for Filipino and European American boys suggesting that they share the same basic dimension of autonomy granting. However, strong invariance was not supported, indicating a lack of scalar equivalence. Thus, values on this scale may not be comparable in these two groups. Filipino and European American girls showed a lack of configural invariance on the measure of autonomy granting because several items did not load significantly on the underlying factor for Filipina Americans. Possibly, these items are not relevant to Filipinas' understanding or experience of autonomy, or perhaps they form different factors reflecting distinct underlying dimensions. A more extensive measure of perceived autonomy granting would be needed to explore group differences in the number of dimensions.

In any case, the lack of configural invariance casts doubt on the utility of this measure in studies of Filipinas and suggests that Filipina and European American girls may have different understandings of autonomy.

Perhaps the most striking finding of the present analysis is the total lack of measurement equivalence observed between Chinese Americans and the other two ethnic groups. The factor structure of all three parenting measures differed for Chinese Americans of both genders such that configural invariance was not supported. Conceptually, the results are consistent with the notion that Chinese American youth hold different concepts of parental support and autonomy granting compared to either European or Filipino American adolescents. This interpretation is consistent with prior research on Chinese parenting which indicates that distinct philosophical traditions underlie Chinese parenting, resulting in different dimensions of parenting and/or a different understanding of particular parenting behaviors (Chao, 1996; Wu & Chao, 2005). The results support the notion that parenting behaviors are embedded in culturally based meaning systems (Greenfield, 1994; Super & Harkness, 1986) and need to be interpreted within those systems in order to be understood. On a practical level, the results indicate that the Add Health parenting measures examined here cannot be used with confidence among Chinese American adolescents of either gender and, moreover, that comparisons of Chinese Americans and other youth based on these measures would be ill-advised.

For Chinese American boys, three maternal support items failed to load on the maternal support factor, and the fit of the one-factor paternal support model was poor; also two items failed to load significantly on the autonomy factor. For Chinese girls, the fit of the one-factor solution for maternal support was poor, and one paternal support item failed to load significantly on the paternal support factor; additionally, two autonomy items did not load on the autonomy factor. The failure of one or more items to load significantly on a factor could mean that each parenting measure comprises multiple dimensions for Chinese American youth (rather than only one) or that certain items are irrelevant to the parenting construct tapped by the measure. In contrast, poor model fit could indicate that there is no coherent pattern in the data. In the present case, an exploratory factor analysis of each parenting measure failed to identify meaningful factors among Chinese American boys or girls. However, the small number of items may have precluded finding multiple distinct dimensions. The question of multiple dimensions should be examined in future studies that employ more extensive measures of perceived maternal and paternal support and autonomy granting.

Nonetheless, examining the items that did not load significantly on the specified factor may be instructive. For Chinese boys, the items for perceived maternal caring, closeness to mother, and maternal warmth failed to load significantly on the maternal support factor. These results suggest that, for boys, the experience of maternal caring, closeness, and warmth are not strongly linked to feelings of satisfaction regarding their relationships with their mothers. Perhaps satisfaction with parent-child relationships among Chinese Americans is distinct from perceptions of warmth and closeness; rather it may depend on other characteristics such as fulfillment of parental role obligations. For Chinese girls, one of the four paternal support items (how much the father cares) failed to load significantly on the paternal support factor. This suggests that a girl's perception that her father cares is distinct from her experience of a supportive father and her satisfaction with the relationship. Perhaps paternal caring is simply assumed or expressed in ways that are unconnected to warmth, feeling close, and satisfaction. The results for both genders are consistent with the notion that direct expressions of warmth and affection are less central to Chinese Americans' conceptions of support (Chao, 2001a; Wu & Chao, 2005). More broadly, the characteristics that define parent-child relationships may be culturally specific, and those assessed in the Add Health measures may be less relevant for Chinese American adolescents compared to their European American and Filipino American counterparts. Taken together, the present findings indicate that the dimensions of parental support reported by Chinese American adolescents differ from those of European American and Filipino adolescents, and this difference deserves further study.

The lack of configural invariance observed between European American girls and both groups of Asian girls on the measure of autonomy granting also merits further attention. For Filipina and Chinese American girls, some items (notably decisions about what to eat) failed to load significantly on the autonomy-granting factor, suggesting that multiple factors could be present or that certain items are irrelevant for measuring the construct. It is also interesting that two items (i.e., those regarding how much TV to watch and bedtimes) did not load significantly for Chinese American boys; perhaps these belong to a separate domain of autonomy.

Although the present study utilized a national data set with representative samples of Chinese American, Filipino American, and European American youth, certain limitations apply. The Add Health sample was based on English-speaking, in-school youth and our analysis was restricted to youth who endorsed a single race and nationality as describing them best. This led us to exclude youth who were Hispanic or who had multiple racial affiliations (e.g., biracial youth who did not identify themselves primarily as White or Asian). Furthermore, we had only adolescent self-report measures, and, although it can be argued that adolescents' perceptions of their parents' behavior are most likely to affect their adjustment (Rohner, 1986), it would be best to triangulate adolescent reports, parent reports, and observer ratings in order to fully capture parents' behavior and the meanings that parents and adolescents attribute to them. Finally, the measures of parenting were relatively brief, and it would be interesting to replicate the present results in studies using more extensive measures. It is important to remember that the present results pertain only to the constructs of parental support and autonomy granting as they were measured in the Add Health study. Aspects of parental support and autonomy granting that are salient to adolescents (especially Asian Americans) may have been omitted, affecting the results.

Despite these limitations, the present results add to the growing body of research on parenting and Asian youth and to the meager literature on measurement equivalence with Asians. Our findings suggest that the understanding of maternal and paternal support may be similar for European and Filipino Americans; furthermore, a shared understanding of autonomy granting seems likely for boys in these two ethnic groups but perhaps not for girls. The results further indicate that Chinese American adolescents in particular may have distinct conceptions of these constructs, which need to be elucidated. Further attention to the cultural bases of parenting practices and parent-adolescent relationships, particularly for Chinese American immigrant families, is needed: this is the focus of the two chapters that follow. To gain a richer understanding of the perspectives of Chinese and Filipino American adolescents on parental support and autonomy granting, it is important to learn how these youth define good parent-adolescent relationships, a topic we turn to in Chapters 5 and 6.

References

Agbayani-Siewert, P. (1994). Filipino American culture and family: Guidelines for practitioners. *Families in Society*, *75*, 429–438.

Bae, W., & Brekke, J. S. (2003). The measurement of self-esteem among Korean Americans: A cross-ethnic study. *Cultural Diversity and Ethnic Minority Psychology*, *9*, 16–33.

Bearman, P. S., Jones, J., & Udry, J. R. (1997). *The national longitudinal study of adolescent health: Research design* [WWW document], http://www.cpc.unc.edu/addhealth

Berndt, T. J., Cheung, P. C., Lau, S., & Hau, K. (1993). Perceptions of parenting in mainland China, Taiwan, and Hong Kong: Sex differences and societal differences. *Developmental Psychology*, *29*, 156–164.

Bond, M., & Wang, S. (1983). Aggressive behaviour in Chinese society: The problem of maintaining order and harmony. *Bulletin of the Hong Kong Psychological Society*, *8*, 5–25.

Byrne, B. M., Shavelson, R. J., & Muthén, B. (1989). Testing for the equivalence of factor covariance and mean structures: The issue of partial measurement invariance. *Psychological Bulletin*, *105*, 456–466.

Chantala, K., & Tabor, J. (1999). *Strategies to perform a design-based analysis using the Add Health data* [WWW document], http://www.cpc.unc.edu/addhealth

Chao, R. K. (1994). Beyond parental control and authoritarian parenting style: Understanding Chinese parenting through the cultural notion of training. *Child Development*, *65*, 1111–1119.

Chao, R. K. (1996). Chinese and European American mothers' beliefs about the role of parenting in children's school success. *Journal of Cross-Cultural Psychology*, *27*, 403–423.

Chao, R. K. (2001a). Extending research on the consequences of parenting style for Chinese Americans and European Americans. *Child Development*, *72*, 1832–1843.

Chiu, L. (1987). Child-rearing attitudes of Chinese American, Chinese American-American, and European-American mothers. *International Journal of Psychology*, *22*, 409–419.

Crockett, L. J., Brown, J., Iturbide, M. I., Russell, S. T., & Wilkinson-Lee, A. (2009). Conceptions of parent–adolescent relationships among Cuban American teenagers. *Sex Roles*, *60*, 575–587.

Crockett, L. J., Brown, J., Russell, S. T., & Shen, Y.-L. (2007). The meaning of good parent–child relationships for Mexican American adolescents. *Journal of Research on Adolescence*, 17, 639–668.

Crockett, L. J., Randall, B. A., Shen, Y., Russell, S. T., & Driscoll, A. K. (2005). Measurement equivalence of the center for epidemiological studies depression scale for Latino and Anglo adolescents: A national study. *Journal of Consulting and Clinical Psychology*, *73*, 47–58.

Fuligni, A. J. (1998). Authority, autonomy, and parent–adolescent conflict and cohesion: A study of adolescents from Mexican, Chinese, Filipino, and European backgrounds. *Developmental Psychology*, *34*, 782–792.

Fuligni, A. J., & Pedersen, S. (2002). Family obligation and the transition to young adulthood. *Developmental Psychology, 38*, 856–868.

Ghorpade, J., Hattrup, K., & Lackritz, J. R. (1999). The use of personality measures in cross-cultural research: A test of three personality scales across two countries. *Journal of Applied Psychology, 84*, 670–679.

Greenfield, P. M. (1994). Independence and interdependence as developmental scripts: Implications for theory, research, and practice. In P. M. Greenfield & R. R. Cocking (Eds.), *Cross-cultural roots of minority child development* (pp. 1–37), Hillsdale, NJ: Lawrence Erlbaum Associates.

Hui, C. H., & Triandis, H. C. (1985). Measurement in cross-cultural psychology. *Journal of Cross-Cultural Psychology, 16*, 131–152.

Jöreskog, K., & Sörbom, D. (1998). *LISREL 8: Structural equation modeling with the SIMPLIS command language*. Lincolnwood, IL: Scientific Software International, Inc.

Julian, T. W., McHenry, P. C., & McKelvey, M. W. (1994). Cultural variations in parenting, perceptions of Caucasian, African American, Hispanic, and Asian American parents. *Family Relations, 43,* 30–37.

Kelloway, E. K. (1998). *Using LISREL for structural equation modeling*. Thousand Oaks, CA: Sage Publications.

Kline, R. B. (1998). *Principles and practice of structural equation modeling*. New York: Guilford Press.

Knight, G. P., & Hill, N. E. (1998). Measurement equivalence in research involving minority adolescents. In V. McLoyd & L. Steinberg (Eds.), *Studying minority adolescents: Conceptual, methodological and theoretical issues* (pp. 183–210). Hillsdale, NJ: Lawrence Erlbaum Associates, Inc.

Lam, C. (2003). Covert parental control: Parent–adolescent interaction and adolescent development in a Chinese American context. *International Journal of Adolescence Medical Health, 15*, 63–77.

Lansford, J. E., Chang, L., Dodge, K. A., Malone, P. S., Oburu, P., Palmerus, K., et al. (2005). Physical discipline and children's adjustment: Cultural normativeness as a moderator. *Child Development, 76*, 1129–1317.

Lau, S. Lew, W. J. F., Hau, K. T., Cheung, P. C., & Berndt, T. J. (1990). Relations among perceived parental control, Warmth, indulgence, and family harmony of Chinese American in mainland China. *Developmental Psychology, 26*, 674–677.

Lin, C. C., & Fu, V. R. (1990). A comparison of child-rearing practices among Chinese American, immigrant Chinese American, and Caucasian-American parents. *Child Development, 61*(2), *Special Issue on Minority Children*, 429–433.

Maruyama, G. M. (1998). *Basics of structural equation modeling*. Thousand Oaks, CA: Sage Publications.

Muthén, L. K., & Muthén, B. O. (1998–2007). *Mplus user's guide* (5th ed.). Los Angeles, CA: Muthén & Muthén.

Nomura, N., Noguchi, Y., Saito, S., & Tezuka, I. (1995). Family characteristics and dynamics in Japan and the United States: A preliminary report from the family environment scale. *International Journal of Intercultural Relations, 19*, 59–86.

Pe-Pua, R., & Protacio-Marcelino, E. (2000). Sikolohiyang Pilipino (Filipino psychology): A legacy of Virgilio G. Enriquez. *Asian Journal of Social Psychology, 3*, 49–71.

Rohner, R. P. (1986). *The warmth dimension: Foundations of parental acceptance-rejection theory*. Thousand Oaks, CA: Sage Publications, Inc.

Super, C. M., & Harkness, S. (1986). The developmental niche: A conceptualization at the interface of child and culture. *International Journal of Behavioral Development, 9*, 545–569.

Udry, J. R. (1998). The national longitudinal study of adolescent health (add health), waves I & II, 1994–1996 [machine-readable data file and documentation]. Chapel Hill, NC: Carolina Population Center, University of North Carolina.

Vandenberg, R. J., & Lance, C. E. (2000). A review and synthesis of the measurement invariance literature: Suggestions, practices, and recommendations for organization research. *Organizational Research Methods*, *3*, 4–70.

Wu, C. X., & Chao, R. K. (2005). Intergenerational cultural conflicts for Chinese American youth with immigrant parents: Norms of parental warmth and the consequences. *International Journal of Behavioral Development*, *29*, 516–523.

Youniss, J., & Smollar, J. (1985). *Adolescents' relations with mothers, fathers, and friends*. Chicago: University of Chicago Press.

Yuan, K. H., & Bentler, P. M. (2000). Three likelihood-based methods for mean and covariance structure analysis with nonnormal missing data. In M. E. Sobel & M. P. Becker (Eds.), *Sociological methodology 2000* (pp. 165–200). Washington, DC: ASA.

Chapter 3
Parental Beliefs and Their Relation to the Parental Practices of Immigrant Chinese Americans and European Americans

Inna A. Padmawidjaja and Ruth K. Chao

In recent decades, ecological theories have become an important basis for research and theory about contemporary family life. These theories are grounded in the idea that individual development takes place within a nested set of ecological contexts; a child grows up in a family, attending schools, which exist within larger communities, each of which is influenced by broader societal influences. According to an ecological-cultural framework, parental practices are an instantiation of parental belief systems (Gallimore, Goldenberg, & Weisner, 1993; Super & Harkness, 1986). These theories offer an understanding of the influence of culture on parenting. Specifically, parental control practices cannot be adequately understood without considering the types of beliefs that parents espouse regarding children. Asian immigrant parents may believe that children need a great deal of guidance throughout their development; thus control is not only necessary, but it is an important *responsibility* of parents. Thus, the practices or features that define parental control for Asian immigrants may differ from those that define the more democratic types of parental control for European Americans due to different cultural meanings ascribed to parenting (Chao, 1994, 2001; Wu & Chao, 2005). In addition, these cultural meanings are manifested in the type of cultural scripts that individuals hold for parenting. Cultural scripts for parenting not only determine how parenting is defined, but also determine the expectations and goals that parents and adolescents have for parenting. Expectations for parenting encompass beliefs about the nature of the child, the child's development, and parents' role in fostering that development (Super & Harkness, 1986). In this chapter we investigate the extent to which immigrant Chinese and European Americans endorse different types of parental behaviors, involving control and responsiveness/support, and how such practices are influenced by their cultural belief systems and parenting goals.

Researchers have provided evidence that many views about the nature of the child emphasized in China and other parts of East Asia have their origins in Confucian sources, particularly the ideas of Mencius. These views have been typified in the

I.A. Padmawidjaja (✉)
University of California, Riverside, CA, USA
e-mail: innapad@gmail.com

S.T. Russell et al. (eds.), *Asian American Parenting and Parent-Adolescent Relationships*, Advancing Responsible Adolescent Development,
DOI 10.1007/978-1-4419-5728-3_3, © Springer Science+Business Media, LLC 2010

analogy that children are "like white paper," emphasizing children's innocence, lack of experience or knowledge, and that children are special and even "divine" (Boocock, 1991; Chao, 2000a; Kojima, 1986). Additionally, these views about the nature of the child are related to parents' views of children's development and parent's role in fostering that development. The importance placed on the parental role is evident in "cultivation" perspectives espoused in many Japanese writings about childhood (Chen, 1996). Chen points out that in Japanese, the word for cultivating a person is the same as that for cultivating plants. The development of children is analogous to the cultivation of a tree that first begins with the seedling. As the tree grows, the grower's care is needed in the trimming of its branches and leaves, but not before the plant's own "inner tendencies" have unfolded. The importance of the parent in providing the proper education to the child, when the child is ready, is essential in starting the child off in the "correct" direction. Children in turn are expected to regard parents and other elders as more knowledgeable authority figures. These views may be contrasted with Western ideologies of the child and the parent's role in fostering the child's development. Western ideologies are largely influenced by the perspectives of child development specialists and researchers. These perspectives often stress a combination of Piagetian views and Western perspectives involving the development of the self and one's identity (Chao, 2000b; Goodnow & Collins, 1990).

Piaget's views of the "child as active learner" emphasize that parents must provide the right amount of stimulation for children, while allowing children to direct their own learning through experimentation and experience. McGillicuddy-De Lisi, De Lisi, Flaugher, and Sigel (1987) have described such an approach as "distancing," in that parents try to encourage avenues for children's own direct interaction with or manipulation of objects or events in the world as a means to foster children's cognitive development. Self-development involves children's exploration of their gender and individual identity. This view holds that parents must be able to recognize, appreciate, and foster children's budding recognition of their own uniqueness, strengths, and potential as an individual (Chao, 1995, 2000b). These views ultimately emphasize children's self-direction.

The parenting practices of Asian immigrants, particularly their parental control strategies, may differ from the control strategies of European American parents due to the different cultural scripts or parental belief systems that inform their practices. Thus, this study is intended to capture cultural distinctions regarding parental practices, as well as parental goals or belief systems. Specifically, in this study, parental control practices will include a more culturally relevant type of control—that of guan—as well as standard measures for behavioral control and responsiveness, based on the Child-rearing Practices Behavioral Inventory (CRPBI) by Schludermann and Schludermann (1988). Applied to adolescents, guan entails a governance and guidance of youth that includes (1) setting expectations for obedience and (2) explaining them, in addition to (3) monitoring the whereabouts of youth. Although adolescents are granted more autonomy relative to younger children due to their increased maturity, immigrant Chinese American parents believe that this autonomy must be balanced with considerations of whether the youth can act responsibly, an approach Chao (2005) has labeled "contingent autonomy."

Thus, for immigrant Chinese American parents, guan includes not only monitoring a youth's whereabouts, but also considerations of whether youth can act responsibly and understand the consequences of their behavior.

Two approaches were undertaken in this study for demonstrating whether each parenting concept has cultural meaning or relevance for Chinese American and European American families. The first focuses on the *endorsement* (i.e., frequency levels) of a particular parental belief system or a set of goals across the two ethnic groups. This endorsement reflects the salience of one particular parenting concept over another for Chinese Americans and European Americans. Specifically, we expect Chinese Americans to endorse parental goals related to Confucian values more than European Americans, and endorse goals for child-centered values less than European Americans. We also expect that Chinese Americans will endorse parental control (that is, behavioral and guan) more than European Americans, and parental warmth less than European Americans. However, in addition, guan will be endorsed to a greater degree than behavioral control among the Chinese American adolescents and their parents. Although Chinese Americans may endorse aspects of behavioral control, particularly monitoring, more than European Americans, these types of control do not capture the central features of their parenting. Their parenting can be described more adequately by the notion of guan. Additionally, analyses will also be conducted comparing adolescents' reports with parents' to determine whether there are greater adolescent-parent discrepancies among Chinese Americans than European Americans, as reported by Wu and Chao (2005) with parental warmth.

The second approach focuses on the *relationships* (i.e., correlational) between parenting goals and parental control, as well as between goals and parental warmth. We expect both types of parental control (behavioral control and guan) to be more strongly related to parenting goals that emphasize Confucian values among Chinese Americans than European Americans. Further, we expect warmth to be more negatively related to Confucian goals, and more positively related to child-centered goals, among European Americans than among Chinese Americans. This study includes both adolescents' and parents' reports of parenting, because parents may not necessarily see their own behaviors in the same way that adolescents do. Adolescents' perceptions of their socialization contexts are of considerable importance because they represent parenting behavior as the adolescent experiences it (Bierman, 1983; Blyth, 1992; Broffenbrenner, 1977). Also, the reliance on multiple informants (adolescents' and parents' report) provides a more complete picture of parenting (Sigel, McGillicudy-DeLisi, & Goodnow, 1992).

Data, Measures, and Methods

Participants

This study included 307 Chinese American-American (116 first-generation and 191 second-generation) and 280 European American-American (primarily third-generation or later) students in the ninth grade and their parents (i.e., the primary caregiver). The samples were recruited from nine different high schools in the Southern California area. Chinese American adolescents' average age was 16.63 years ($SD = 0.61$) and European American adolescents' average age was 16.59 ($SD = 0.65$). Of the first-generation Chinese American immigrant youth, 44.8% were from Taiwan, 39.7% were from People's Republic of China, and 15.5% were from Hong Kong. The parents of the first generation of Chinese American reported that they were from Taiwan (40%), Republic of China (38%), and Hong Kong (10%), with the remainder from other parts of Asia. Of the parents of the second-generation youth, 53% were from Taiwan, 17% were from People's Republic of China, 7% were from Hong Kong, and the remainder from other parts of Asia. The first-generation immigrant adolescents came to live in the United States at an average age of 7.56 years. Means or proportions and standard deviations of adolescent and family characteristics are presented in Table 3.1.

Table 3.1 Means or proportions, and (standard deviation or standard errors) on adolescent, parent and family characteristics for each ethnic group

	Chinese Americans (%)	European Americans (%)	Differences across ethnic groups
Adolescent's gender (female)	$N = 306$ 54.2%	$N = 275$ 47.6%	$\chi^2(1) = 2.53, p = 0.11$
Primary caregiver (mother)	$N = 302$ 86.4%	$N = 275$ 81.5%	$\chi^2(1) = 2.62, p = 0.10$
Single parenthood	$N = 307$ 10.7%	$N = 280$ 9.6%	$\chi^2(1) = 0.20, p = 0.66$
Home ownership	$N = 297$ 83.8%	$N = 277$ 78.3%	$\chi^2(1) = 2.84, p = 0.09$
	Mean (SD)	Mean (SD)	
Mother's education	$N = 305$ 6.82 (1.52)	$N = 277$ 6.75 (1.36)	n.s.
Father's education	$N = 307$ 6.98 (1.23)	$N = 280$ 6.71 (1.28)	E < C
Parent's income	$N = 307$ 4.31 (1.33)	$N = 280$ 4.80 (1.23)	C < E

Note: C = Chinese Americans and E = European Americans; the findings for the across-group differences were based on an alpha level of 0.05. For education level, a score of 6 = "some college or vocational training," and 7 = "finished 2-year community college degree;" for income level, a score of 4 = "between US $50,000 and just under US $75,000," 5 = "between US $75,000 and just under US $100,000," and 6 = " over US $100,000."

Procedure

Adolescents. In order to allow adolescents' participation in the study, parents were mailed an information letter explaining the study, with a pre-addressed enclosed response form that they could send back if they did *not* wish their child to participate.

All parents received copies of the information letter in English and Chinese. After parental consent was acquired, adolescents were provided with an assent statement on the cover page of their survey that informed them about the study, that their participation was voluntary, and that they could choose not to answer any of the questions. Adolescents were given 50 min (the whole class period) to complete paper-and-pencil surveys. The participation rate was quite high, at 77.4%. Of all adolescents eligible to participate (i.e., those in the ninth grade), fewer than 12.6% either refused to participate or did not have parental consent; while another 10% were either absent on the day of the study or did not receive the parental information letter.

Parents. Parents of adolescents with completed surveys were mailed a recruitment letter in English, Chinese, and Korean informing them that we would be contacting them to participate in a telephone survey and that they would receive US $30 for participating. Those parents who were identified by the adolescents as the primary caregiver were then contacted by telephone, and were provided with a consent statement that informed them about the study, that their participation was voluntary, and that they could choose not to answer any of the questions. Parent surveys were conducted by telephone in the respondents' preferred language, and parents were paid US $30 for participating. The participation rate for parents (i.e., the primary caregiver) was a bit lower than adolescents at 63.3%. Of all parents eligible to participate (i.e., those identified as the primary caregiver and who had completed adolescent surveys), fewer than 36.7% either refused to participate or could not be reached.

Translation of surveys. All of the parent measures were translated into Chinese and back-translated, as in previous studies (Chao, 2000a; Chao & Tran, 2000). First, all measures were translated into Chinese American by at least two bilingual translators for each language; this version was then translated back into English by another two bilingual translators. Both translators and back-translators compared this back-translated English version with the original English version to resolve any discrepancies in the two versions, and changes were made to the translations based on their resolutions.

Measures

Behavioral control. Adolescents' reports of parental behavioral control were captured by the firm control subscale of the CRPBI (Schaefer, 1965), as adapted by Schludermann and Schludermann (1988). The scale contains ten items that assess the degree to which adolescents perceived their parents as setting standards and expectations, and enforcing them (e.g., "Gives hard punishment when I misbehave"). The corresponding parent-reported measure was similarly worded (e.g., "Gives hard punishment when he/she misbehave").

Guan. Adolescents' and parents' reports of guan were captured by the guan parental control scale (Chao & Wu, 2001). The scale consists of 12 items that assess the degree to which adolescents perceive their parents as setting standards and expectations (e.g., "Expects me to follow his/her wishes"), explaining and making standards very clear (e.g., "Explains to me what he/she expects from me"), and monitoring and giving autonomy only when youth act responsibly, also described above as "Contingent Autonomy" (e.g., "Gives me more freedom only if I show (her/him) that I am responsible."). The corresponding parent-reported measure was similarly worded (e.g., "Expect him/her to follow my wishes).

Warmth. Adolescents' and parents' reports of parental warmth were captured by the acceptance-rejection subscale of the CRPBI as adapted by Schludermann and Schludermann (1988). The subscale consisted of ten items that assess the degree to which adolescents perceive their parents as responsive and warm (e.g., "Gives me a lot of care and attention"). The corresponding parent-reported measure was similarly worded (e.g., "Give him/her a lot of care and attention").

For all three subscales describe above, responses to the items completed by adolescents were coded on a 5-point scale ranging from 1 (*not at all like*) to 5 (*a lot like*), and those completed by parents were coded on a 5-point scale ranging from 1 (*strongly disagree*) to 5 (*strongly agree*).

In order to determine whether each of the parenting scales described above would form one scale or separate subscales, factor analyses were conducted for each scale for adolescents and parents separately using varimax rotation with the criterion that all items load at 0.40 or above (Guadagnoli & Velicer, 1988). With the *behavioral control* items, a two-factor structure was found to be most consistent across adolescents and parents. The first factor, labeled Restricted Autonomy (three items, e.g., "Gives me as much freedom as I want (reverse)"), had adequate internal consistencies across adolescents ($\alpha = 0.74$ for Chinese American, and $\alpha = 0.78$ for European American), but weak consistencies across parents ($\alpha = 0.55$ for Chinese American, and $\alpha = 0.58$ for European American). The second factor, labeled Strictness (three items, e.g., "Is very strict with me"), had adequate internal consistencies across adolescents ($\alpha = 0.75$ for Chinese American, and $\alpha = 0.70$ for European American), but weaker consistencies across parents, particularly for Chinese Americans ($\alpha = 0.55$ for Chinese American, and $\alpha = 0.67$ for European American).

With the guan items, a three-factor structure was found to be most consistent across adolescents and parents. The first factor, labeled Contingent Autonomy (three items, e.g., "Watches how I behave before giving me more freedom"), had good internal consistency across adolescents ($\alpha = 0.81$ for Chinese American, and $\alpha = 0.75$ for European American), and somewhat weaker consistencies across parents ($\alpha = 0.65$ for Chinese American, and $\alpha = 0.72$ for European American). The second factor, labeled Expects Obedience (three items, e.g., "Tells me to follow her/his wishes"), had adequate internal consistencies across adolescents ($\alpha = 0.76$ for Chinese American, and $\alpha = 0.68$ for European American), but weaker consistencies across parents, particularly European Americans ($\alpha = 0.63$ for Chinese American, and $\alpha = 0.43$ for European American). Because the third factor, labeled Explains Obedience ("Explains to me what s/he expects from me" and "Tells me what she/he thinks is best for me"), consisted of only two items it had somewhat weak internal consistencies across adolescents ($\alpha = 0.60$ for Chinese American, and $\alpha = 0.61$ for European American), and very weak consistencies across parents ($\alpha = 0.32$ for Chinese American, and $\alpha = 0.15$ for European American). With the warmth items, four of the original ten items consistently loaded on one factor across adolescents, with excellent internal consistencies ($\alpha = 0.87$ for Chinese American, and $\alpha = 0.89$ for European American), and adequate consistencies for parents ($\alpha = 0.62$ for Chinese American, and $\alpha = 0.71$ for European American). Based on these factor structures, scale scores were created by calculating the mean of the items. Thus, it appears that the scales for behavioral control, guan, and warmth may be more reliable for adolescents than for parents, and this is consistent for both Chinese Americans and European Americans.

Parental beliefs. Parents' beliefs were measured by parents' reports of their socialization goals based on Chao's (2001) Confucian and Child-centered goals for child rearing. The scale, developed for this study, consisted of 26 items that assess Confucian goals stressing the importance of *perseverance*, *working hard in school*, *being obedient*, and *being sensitive to parents' wishes* (e.g., "To respect their elders" and "To always put their schoolwork/education first"), Child-centered goals stressing the importance of independence and self-expression (e.g., "To be unique and their own individual" and "To be self-expressive and verbal"). Responses were coded on a 4-point scale ranging from 1 (*not at all desired*) to 4 (*very strongly desired*). All items were then subjected to a factor analysis with a varimax rotation; items with loadings of 0.40 above were selected. Two factors seemed to be evident for both Chinese American and European American parents with five items capturing the Confucian goals ($\alpha = 0.83$ for Chinese American and $\alpha = 0.81$ for European Americans), and five items capturing the Child-centered goals ($\alpha = 0.82$ for Chinese American and $\alpha = 0.77$ for European Americans). Separate scale scores were created for each subscale, Confucian and Child-centered goals, by averaging the items of each subscale.

Adolescent and family characteristics. Adolescents reported their gender (1 = "female"; 0 = "male") and *primary caregiver* (1 = "mother," 2 = "father," 3 = "step-mother," 4 = "step-father," and 5 ="other"). The *parent's education*, also based on adolescents' reports, was created by averaging the mean of mother's and father's education, which was based on an item asking what is the highest level of education attained (1 = "no formal schooling," 2 = "some elementary school," 3 = "finished elementary school," 4 = "finished middle school," "finished high school," 5 = "some vocational or college training," 6 = "finished 4-year college degree," and 7 = "finished graduate degree"). *Single parenthood* was assessed through an item asking youth with whom they lived, with those youth who indicated "only my mother" or "only my father" coded as 1 and all others coded as 0. Finally, *home ownership* was assessed with the following question: "Do your parents own the home you live in?" (1 = "yes," 0 = "no").

Results

Means/proportions and standard deviations of adolescents' and family characteristics are presented in Table 3.1 for each ethnic group. As Table 3.1 shows, although Chinese American-American fathers had significantly higher levels of education ($M = 6.98$, $SD = 1.23$) than European American fathers ($M = 6.71$, $SD = 1.28$),

$t(585) = 2.68$, $p < 0.01$, Chinese American-American parents had significantly lower levels of income ($M = 4.31$, $SD = 1.33$) than their European American counterparts ($M = 4.80$, $SD = 1.23$), $t(585) = -4.62$, $p < 0.01$.

Differences in Mean Levels or Proportion

The means and standard deviations of the parenting practices and goals reported by adolescents and parents for each ethnic group are presented in Table 3.2. Separate multivariate analyses were conducted for adolescents' and parents' reports to test whether there were ethnic group differences in parenting practices and goals. One-way MANOVAs were used with the six parental measures as dependent variables: Restricted Autonomy, Strictness, Contingent Autonomy, Expects Obedience, Explains Obedience, and warmth. This multivariate test yielded a significant ethnic group effect, based on both adolescent report $F(8, 561) = 9.33$, $p < 0.01$, and parent report, $F(9, 576) = 61.31$, $p < 0.01$. These analyses were then followed by post hoc *t*-test comparisons across the two ethnic groups for adolescents' and then parents' reports.

Then, in order to determine whether discrepancies between adolescents' and parents' reports of parenting would be greater for Chinese Americans than European Americans, discrepancy scores were calculated by subtracting the parents' reports of their practices from that reported by adolescents. *T*-tests across the two ethnic groups on these discrepancy scores were then conducted. Ethnic differences were found in the discrepancy scores of Strictness, Expects Obedience, and warmth, $t(579) = 3.32$, $p < 0.01$, $t(577) = 2.75$, $p < 0.01$, and $t(578) = -3.15$, $p < 0.01$, respectively, with Chinese Americans reporting higher discrepancies than European Americans. Ethnic differences in the discrepancy scores of Restricted Autonomy were also found, $t(578) = -7.91$, $p < 0.01$, with Chinese Americans having *lower* discrepancies than European Americans. In the following sections, results for ethnic differences are presented for each parenting variable, which are summarized first, followed by results on parent-adolescent differences within each ethnic group.

Parent reports of Confucian and child-centered goals. Differences across ethnic groups on the Confucian and Child-centered goals were found [$t(585) = 11.72$, $p < 0.01$, $t(585) = -2.05$, $p < 0.05$, respectively], with Chinese American parents endorsing the Confucian goals more than the European Americans, and European Americans endorsing the child-centered goals more than the Chinese Americans.

Adolescent & parent reports of restricted autonomy. Based on *parents'* reports only, there were mean differences in Restricted Autonomy across ethnic groups, $t(585) = -10.17$, $p < 0.01$, with Chinese American parents reporting less Restricted Autonomy than their European American counterparts. Then, in comparisons between adolescents and their parents, differences were found among European Americans, $t(274) = -12.23$, $p < 0.01$, with adolescents reporting lower levels than parents. Taken together these findings mean that Chinese American and European American youth report similar levels of Restricted Autonomy for their parents,

Table 3.2 Means and standard deviations on parental goals and practices variables reported by adolescents and parents

	Chinese Americans			European Americans			
	Adolescent mean (SD)	Parent mean (SD)	r	Adolescent mean (SD)	Parent mean (SD)	r	Tests for differences across ethnic groups
Confucian goals	–	$N = 307$ 2.61 (0.53)	–	–	$N = 280$ 2.09 (0.56)	–	(P) E < C
Child-centered goals	–	$N = 307$ 3.03 (0.45)	–	–	$N = 280$ 3.11 (0.49)	–	(P) C < E
Restricted autonomy (1)	$N = 306$ 3.72 (0.82)	$N = 307$ 3.80 (0.80)	$N = 306$ 0.18**	$N = 274$ 3.67 (0.90)	$N = 280$ 4.42(0.68)	$N = 274$. 021**	(P) C < E
Strictness (2)	$N = 304$ 3.08 (0.92)	$N = 307$ 3.34 (0.95)	$N = 304$ 0.16**	$N = 275$ 2.77 (0.83)	$N = 280$ 2.77 (0.97)	$N = 275$ 0.33**	(A) E < C; (P) E < C
Contingent autonomy (3)	$N = 302$ 3.30(0.86)	$N = 306$ 4.29 (0.70)	$N = 301$ –0.07	$N = 274$ 3.27 (0.83)	$N = 280$ 4.34 (0.72)	$N = 274$ 0.14*	n.s
Explains obedience (4)	$N = 306$ 3.86 (0.83)	$N = 307$ 4.61 (0.56)	$N = 306$ 0.04	$N = 275$ 3.69 (0.88)	$N = 280$ 4.43 (0.53)	$N = 275$ 0.06	(A) E < C; (P) E < C
Expects obedience (5)	$N = 305$ 3.32 (0.93)	$N = 307$ 3.17 (0.95)	$N = 305$ 0.18**	$N = 275$ 3.14 (0.83)	$N = 280$ 3.31 (0.87)	$N = 275$ 0.21**	(A) E < C
Warmth (6)	$N = 306$ 3.25 (1.00)	$N = 307$ 4.61 (0.46)	$N = 306$ 0.11*	$N = 274$ 3.73 (0.96)	$N = 280$ 4.41 (0.53)	$N = 274$ 0.22**	(A) C < E; (P) E< C
Adolescent-Parent differences	(1) n.s.; (2) A< P; (3) A< P; (4) A<P; (5) P < A; (6) A < P			(1) A<P; (2) n.s.; (3) A < P; (4) A<P; (5) A <P; (6) A < P			

*$p < 0.05$; **$p < 0.01$

Note: r = bivariate correlations between adolescent's and parent's reports; A = Adolescents and P = Parents; C = Chinese Americans and E = European Americans.

but European American parents report higher levels for themselves than their adolescents do, and also higher levels than Chinese American parents do.

Adolescent and parent reports of strictness. Mean differences in Strictness across ethnic groups were found [$t(577) = 4.32$, $p < 0.01$, and $t(585) = 7.11$, $p < 0.01$, respectively], with Chinese American adolescents *and* their parents reporting lower levels than their European American counterparts. Then, in looking at differences between adolescents and their parents for each ethnic group separately, differences were found among Chinese Americans [$t(304) = -3.73$, $p < 0.01$], with adolescents reporting lower levels than parents.

Adolescent and parent reports of guan: Contingent autonomy. Based on both adolescent and parent reports, mean differences in Contingent Autonomy across ethnic group were not found. In comparisons between adolescents and their parents, differences were found among Chinese Americans [$t(301) = -15.10$, $p < 0.01$] and among European Americans [$t(274) = -17.33$, $p < 0.01$], with parents reporting higher levels than their adolescents in both ethnic groups.

Adolescent and parent reports of guan: Explains obedience. Mean differences in Explains Obedience across ethnic groups were found [$t(579) = 2.52$, $p < 0.01$, and, $t(585) = 4.08$, $p < 0.01$ respectively], with Chinese American adolescents and their parents reporting higher levels than their European American counterparts. Then, in looking at differences between adolescents and their parents for each ethnic group, differences were found among Chinese Americans [$t(306) = -13.17$, $p < 0.01$], and among European Americans [$t(275) = -12.24$, $p < 0.01$], with parents reporting higher levels than adolescents in both ethnic groups.

Adolescent and parent reports of guan: Expects obedience. Based on adolescents' reports only, mean differences in Expects Obedience across ethnic groups were found, $t(578) = 2.40$, $p < 0.05$, with Chinese American adolescents reporting higher levels than European American adolescents. Then, in the comparisons between adolescents and their parents, differences were found among Chinese Americans [$t(305) = 2.15$, $p < 0.05$], with adolescents reporting higher levels than parents, and among European Americans [$t(275) = -2.34$, $p < 0.05$], with adolescents reporting *lower* levels than parents.

Adolescent and parent reports of warmth. Differences across ethnic groups on parental warmth were found [$t(578) = -5.91$, $p < 0.01$, and, $t(585) = 4.93$, $p < 0.01$, respectively] with Chinese American youth reporting less warmth than European American youth, and Chinese American *parents* reporting *more* warmth than European American parents. Then looking at differences between adolescents and their parents for each ethnic group, differences were found among Chinese Americans [$t(306) = -22.57$, $p < 0.01$], and among European Americans [$t(274) = -11.33$, $p < 0.01$], with parents reporting higher levels of warmth than adolescents in both ethnic groups. Thus, Chinese Americans endorse only one facet of behavioral control, Strictness, and two of three dimensions of guan, Explains and also Expects Obedience, more than European Americans.

Comparisons Across Types of Control

Although Chinese Americans may endorse Strictness, and Explains and Expects Obedience to a greater extent than European Americans, analyses were also conducted to determine which type of control Chinese Americans endorsed most. In order to address whether control defined by guan was emphasized more by Chinese immigrant families than other types of control, separate MANOVAs were first conducted for adolescents and parents, and both *F*-tests were significant [guan: $F(5, 297) = 99.43, p < 0.01$; behavioral control: $F(5, 301) = 262.92, p < 0.01$]. Then separate post hoc analyses were conducted for Chinese American adolescents and their parents, based on *dependent* sample *t*-tests ($p < 0.05$), pairing the scores for each of the three components of guan (i.e., Contingent Autonomy, Expects Obedience, and Explains Obedience) with the two components of behavioral control (i.e., Restricted Autonomy and Strictness). Once again, refer to Table 3.2 for the means and standard deviations of adolescents and parents of both ethnic groups. For Chinese American adolescents, only the component of Explains Obedience was consistently higher than both components of behavioral control; Contingent Autonomy was higher than Strictness, but was lower than the Restricted Autonomy. For Chinese immigrant parents, two of the guan components, Contingent Autonomy and Explains Obedience were consistently higher than both components of behavioral control, but the third component of guan, Expects Obedience, was lower than both components of behavioral control. Thus, it appears that Chinese immigrant *parents* reported using guan more than behavioral control, but this was only for two components of guan, Contingent Autonomy and Explains Obedience. Similar analyses were also conducted for the European American adolescents and parents separately. Summarizing across European American adolescents and parents, Restricted Autonomy was the only component of behavioral control rated higher than guan (for two components, Contingent Autonomy and Expects Obedience), and Strictness was rated lower than all three components of guan.

Associations Between Parents' Beliefs or Goals and Their Practices

In order to examine the associations between parental goals and practices, Pearson's correlations were first conducted within each ethnic group; results are presented in Table 3.3 for Confucian goals and Table 3.4 for child-centered goals. Correlations between the two types of goals were stronger for the immigrant Chinese parents ($r = 0.32, p < 0.01$) than they were for the European American parents ($r = 0.13, p < 0.05$; not shown in Tables 3.3 and 3.4). Next, multiple regression analyses were conducted with both the Confucian and child-centered goals together in the models predicting parenting practices. Ethnic group differences in the associations between parental goals and practices were tested by estimating interactions between ethnicity

Table 3.3 Bivariate associations (r) between Confucian goals and parental practices reported by adolescents and parents

	Chinese Americans		European Americans	
	Adolescents	Parents	Adolescents	Parents
Restricted autonomy	0.02 ($N = 306$)	0.10# ($N = 307$)	–0.04 ($N = 274$)	–0.03 ($N = 280$)
Strictness	0.10 ($N = 304$)	0.33** ($N = 307$)	–0.00 ($N = 274$)	0.20** ($N = 280$)
Contingent autonomy	–0.00 ($N = 302$)	0.19** ($N = 306$)	–0.05 ($N = 274$)	0.11 ($N = 280$)
Explains obedience	0.14* ($N = 306$)	0.25** ($N = 307$)	–0.04 ($N = 275$)	0.18** ($N = 280$)
Expects obedience	0.19** ($N = 305$)	0.46** ($N = 307$)	0.03 ($N = 275$)	0.28** ($N = 280$)
Warmth	–0.04 ($N = 306$)	–0.01 ($N = 307$)	–0.05 ($N = 274$)	0.07 ($N = 280$)

#$p<0.10$
*$p < 0.05$
**$p < 0.01$

Table 3.4 Bivariate associations (r) between Child-centered goals, and parental practices reported by adolescents and parents

	Chinese Americans		European Americans	
	Adolescents	Parents	Adolescents	Parents
Restricted autonomy	–0.02 ($N = 306$)	0.05 ($N = 307$)	–0.15* ($N = 274$)	–0.02 ($N = 280$)
Strictness	0.00 ($N = 304$)	0.10 ($N = 307$)	–0.04 ($N = 276$)	–0.03 ($N = 280$)
Contingent autonomy	0.06 ($N = 302$)	0.25** ($N = 306$)	–0.04 ($N = 274$)	–0.06 ($N = 280$)
Explains obedience	0.05 ($N = 306$)	0.04 ($N = 307$)	–0.04 ($N = 275$)	0.06 ($N = 280$)
Expects obedience	0.03 ($N = 305$)	–0.00 ($N = 307$)	–0.07 ($N = 275$)	–0.14* ($N = 280$)
Warmth	0.04 ($N = 306$)	0.15** ($N = 307$)	0.13* ($N = 274$)	0.26** ($N = 280$)

*$p < 0.05$; **$p < 0.01$

(1 = Chinese American, 0 = European American) and each of the parental goals, Confucian and Child-centered. Significant interactions were interpreted using the following steps. First, simple regression lines were plotted for each ethnic group. For purposes of graphing the interaction, high levels of Confucian goals or Child-centered goals were defined as one standard deviation above the mean, medium levels were at the mean, and low levels were one standard deviation below the mean. Second, the significance of the slopes for these simple regression lines were tested based on Cohen, Cohen, West, and Aiken's test of simple slopes (2003). All the

regression analyses controlled for adolescent's gender, parental education, home ownership, single parent households, and household income.

Adolescent & parent reports of restricted autonomy. Based on both adolescents' and parents' reports, no significant ethnic group differences were found in the associations between the Confucian or Child-centered beliefs, and Restricted Autonomy (see first half of Table 3.5). Therefore, the results reported are for the overall sample. Based on adolescent reports, a negative association was found between the *Child-centered* goals and Restricted Autonomy, net of all other factors [$B = -0.18$, $SE = 0.08$, $p < 0.05$]. On the other hand, based on *parents*' reports, a negative association was found between Confucian goals and Restricted Autonomy, net of all other factors [$B = -0.17$, $SE = 0.06$, $p < 0.01$].

Adolescent & parent reports of strictness. Based on both adolescents' and parents' reports, no significant ethnic group differences were found in the associations between Confucian or child-centered beliefs, and Strictness (see second half of Table 3.5). Therefore, the results are reported for the sample as a whole. Based on both adolescents' and parents' reports, positive associations were found between Confucian goals and Strictness, net of all other factors, [$B = 0.18$, $SE = 0.06$, $p < 0.01$] and [$B = 0.60$, $SE = 0.07$, $p < 0.01$], respectively.

Adolescent & parent reports of guan: Contingent autonomy. Based on adolescents' reports, no significant ethnic differences were found in the associations between Confucian or child-centered goals and Contingent Autonomy (see Table 3.6). Additionally, no associations were found in the sample as a whole.

Based on parents' reports, though, significant ethnic group differences in the associations between child-centered beliefs and Contingent Autonomy were found (fourth through sixth columns in Table 3.6). Compared to European American parents, child-centered goals were more strongly associated with Contingent Autonomy for Chinese American parents. Looking within this latter group, this association was positive [$B = 0.38$, $SE = 0.11$, $t(561) = 3.50$, $p < 0.01$], whereas no association was found for European American parents, as indicated by the main effect of child-centered goals. These associations for each ethnic group are graphically displayed in Fig. 3.1. As no ethnic group differences were found in the association between Confucian goals and Contingent Autonomy, analyses were then conducted on the overall sample. From the overall sample, parents' reports of their Confucian goals were positively related to their Contingent Autonomy [$B = 0.13$, $SE = 0.05$, $p < 0.01$].

Adolescent & parent report of guan: Expects obedience. Based on adolescents' reports, significant ethnic group differences in the associations between Confucian beliefs and Expects Obedience were found (see first half of Table 3.7). Compared to European American adolescents, Confucian goals were more strongly associated with Expects Obedience for Chinese American adolescents, and looking within this latter group, this association was positive [$B = 0.38$, $SE = 0.14$, $t(559) = 2.71$, $p < 0.01$]. However, no association between Confucian goals and Expects Obedience was found for European American youth, as indicated by the main effect of Confucian goals. These associations for each ethnic group are graphically displayed in Fig. 3.2.

Table 3.5 Multiple regressions of ethnicity, family characteristics, parenting goals and interaction terms for ethnicity and parenting goals on behavioral control subscales

	Behavioral control: restricted autonomy						Behavioral control: strictness					
	Adolescents[a]			Parents[b]			Adolescents[c]			Parents[d]		
	B	*SE*	*Sig.*	*B*	*SE*	*Sig.*	*B*	*SE*	*Sig.*	*B*	*SE*	*Sig.*
Adolescent gender (female)	0.11	0.07	0.15	0.01	0.06	0.99	−0.12	0.08	0.10	−0.08	0.08	0.30
Primary caregiver (mother)	0.15	0.10	0.15	0.30	0.09	0.00	0.01	0.10	0.98	0.05	0.11	0.66
Parent's education	0.01	0.01	0.91	0.01	0.01	0.21	−0.01	0.01	0.45	0.01	0.01	0.37
Home ownership	−0.06	0.10	0.55	−0.01	0.09	0.90	0.05	0.10	0.66	0.13	0.11	0.21
Single parenthood	−0.13	0.13	0.30	−0.09	0.11	0.42	−0.24	0.13	0.06	0.21	0.14	0.88
Parent's income	0.05	0.03	0.10	−0.02	0.03	0.56	−0.01	0.03	0.74	−0.03	0.03	0.44
Confucian goals	−0.01	0.10	0.99	−0.01	0.08	0.93	−0.03	0.10	0.79	0.38	0.10	0.00
Child-centered goals	−0.28	0.11	0.01	−0.05	0.09	0.57	−0.03	0.11	0.76	−0.12	0.12	0.31
Ethnicity (Chinese)	−0.64	0.53	0.23	−1.33	0.46	0.00	−0.11	0.55	0.85	−0.65	0.57	0.26

Table 3.5 (continued)

	Behavioral control: restricted autonomy						Behavioral control: strictness					
	Adolescents[a]			Parents[b]			Adolescents[c]			Parents[d]		
	B	*SE*	*Sig.*	*B*	*SE*	*Sig.*	*B*	*SE*	*Sig.*	*B*	*SE*	*Sig.*
Ethnicity (Chinese) × Confucian	0.05	0.14	0.70	0.16	0.12	0.17	0.21	0.14	0.13	0.22	0.15	0.14
Ethnicity (Chinese) × Child-centered	0.18	0.16	0.28	0.09	0.14	0.53	−0.04	0.17	0.80	0.14	0.17	0.43

[a] $N = 563$, $R^2 = 0.03$, $F(11, 551) = 1.45$, $p = 0.15$
[b] $N = 566$, $R^2 = 0.17$, $F(11, 554) = 10.43$, $p < 0.01$
[c] $N = 562$, $R^2 = 0.05$, $F(11, 550) = 2.50$, $p < 0.01$
[d] $N = 566$, $R^2 = 0.16$, $F(11, 554) = 9.66$, $p < 0.01$

Table 3.6 Multiple regressions of ethnicity, family characteristics, parenting goals and interaction terms for ethnicity and parenting goals on first subscale for guan

	Guan: Contingent autonomy					
	Adolescents[a]			Parents[b]		
	B	*SE*	*Sig.*	*B*	*SE*	*Sig.*
Adolescent gender (female)	0.04	0.07	0.59	0.03	0.06	0.59
Primary caregiver (mother)	−0.08	0.10	0.43	0.14	0.08	0.09
Parent's education	−0.01	0.01	0.44	0.01	0.01	0.30
Home ownership	0.03	0.10	0.78	0.05	0.08	0.54
Single parenthood	0.04	0.13	0.78	0.01	0.10	0.94
Parent's income	0.02	0.03	0.63	−0.03	0.03	0.22
Confucian goals	−0.06	0.10	0.55	0.18	0.08	0.02
Child-centered goals	−0.05	0.11	0.63	−0.10	0.09	0.27
Ethnicity (Chinese)	−0.47	0.53	0.38	−1.59	0.43	0.00
Ethnicity (Chinese) × Confucian	0.01	0.14	0.99	−0.2	0.11	0.83
Ethnicity (Chinese) × Child-centered	0.17	0.16	0.29	0.48	0.13	0.00

[a] $N = 559, R^2 = 0.01, F(11, 547) = 0.38, p = 0.97$
[b] $N = 565, R^2 = 0.07, F(11, 553) = 3.56, p < 0.01$

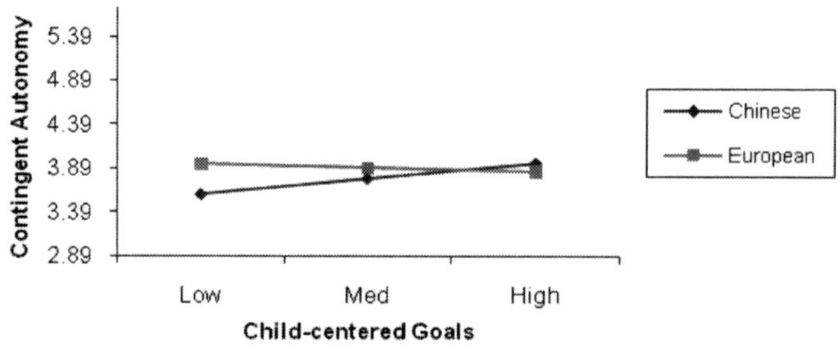

Fig. 3.1 The interactive effect of ethnicity and Child-centered goals on contingent autonomy reported by parent

Based on parents' reports, significant ethnic group differences in the association between Confucian beliefs and Expects Obedience were also found (see fourth through sixth columns in Table 3.7). These beliefs/goals were more strongly associated with Expects Obedience among Chinese Americans than European Americans, although, in looking within each ethnic group, these associations were positive among both groups [European Americans, $B = 0.49$, $SE = 0.09$, $p < 0.01$; and Chinese Americans, $B = 0.90$, $SE = 0.09$, $t(562) = 10.70$, $p < 0.01$]. These associations for each ethnic group are graphically displayed in Fig. 3.3.

Adolescent & parent reports of guan: Explains obedience. Based on adolescents' reports, significant ethnic group differences in the associations between Confucian beliefs and Explains Obedience were found (see second half of Table 3.7). Compared to European American adolescents, Confucian goals were more strongly associated with Explains Obedience for Chinese American adolescents, and looking

Table 3.7 Multiple regressions of ethnicity, family characteristics, parenting goals and interaction terms for ethnicity and parenting goals on second and third subscales for guan

	Guan: Expects obedience						Guan: Explains obedience					
	Adolescents[a]			Parents[b]			Adolescents[c]			Parents[d]		
	B	*SE*	*Sig.*	*B*	*SE*	*Sig.*	*B*	*SE*	*Sig.*	*B*	*SE*	*Sig.*
Adolescent gender (female)	−0.18	0.08	0.02	−0.22	0.07	0.00	0.04	0.07	0.59	−0.03	0.05	0.59
Primary caregiver (mother)	0.12	0.10	0.26	0.07	0.10	0.46	0.02	0.10	0.81	0.03	0.06	0.63
Parent's education	−0.01	0.01	0.11	0.01	0.01	0.43	−0.02	0.01	0.06	0.01	0.01	0.17
Home ownership	0.19	0.10	0.06	0.14	0.09	0.15	0.11	0.10	0.28	0.06	0.06	0.32
Single parenthood	0.01	0.13	0.99	0.06	0.12	0.59	0.13	0.12	0.29	0.10	0.08	0.18
Parent's income	0.01	0.03	0.78	−0.07	0.03	0.02	0.08	0.03	0.01	−0.02	0.02	0.24
Confucian goals	0.05	0.10	0.64	0.49	0.09	0.00	−0.06	0.10	0.51	0.18	0.06	0.00
Child-centered goals	−0.08	0.11	0.45	−0.26	0.10	0.01	−0.07	0.11	0.54	0.03	0.07	0.62
Ethnicity (Chinese)	−0.73	0.54	0.18	−1.30	0.51	0.01	−0.63	0.53	0.24	0.08	0.33	0.80
Ethnicity (Chinese) × Confucian	0.33	0.14	0.02	0.41	0.13	0.00	0.30	0.14	0.03	0.07	0.09	0.42
Ethnicity (Chinese) × Child-centered	−0.01	0.16	0.99	−0.07	0.16	0.68	0.03	0.16	0.87	−0.06	0.10	0.53

[a] $N = 563$, $R^2 = 0.06$, $F(11, 551) = 2.94$, $p < 0.01$
[b] $N = 566$, $R^2 = 0.22$, $F(11, 554) = 13.85$, $p < 0.01$
[c] $N = 564$, $R^2 = 0.05$, $F(11, 552) = 2.53$, $p < 0.01$
[d] $N = 566$, $R^2 = 0.09$, $F(11, 554) = 4.77$, $p < 0.01$

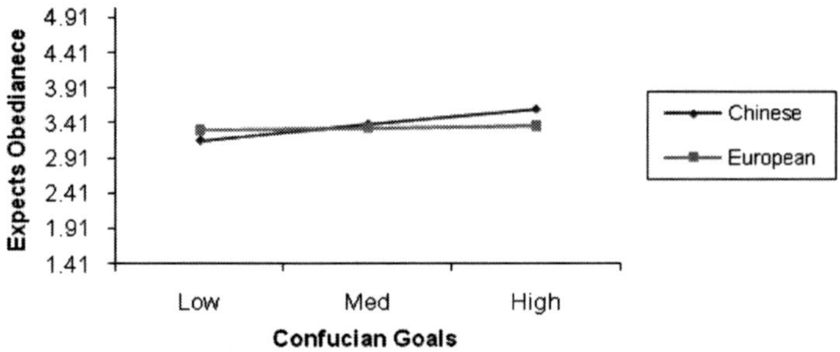

Fig. 3.2 The interactive effect of ethnicity and Confucian goals on expects obedience reported by adolescents

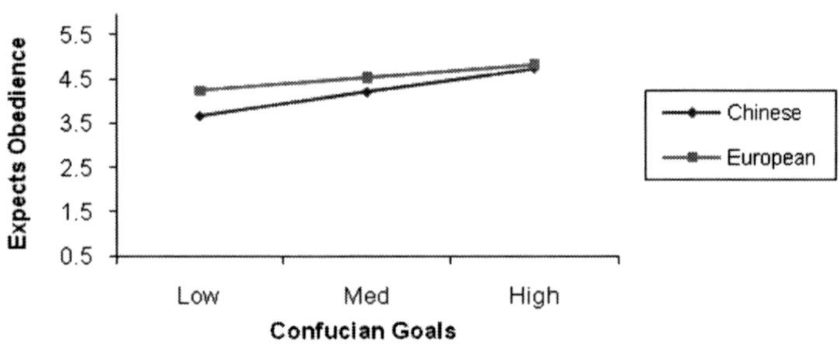

Fig. 3.3 The interactive effect of ethnicity and Confucian goals on expects obedience reported by parent

within this latter group this association was positive [$B = 0.24$, $SE = 0.11$, $t(560)= 2.18$, $p < 0.01$]. However, no association between Confucian goals and Explains Obedience was found for European American youth, as indicated by the main effect of Confucian goals. These associations for each ethnic group are graphically displayed in Fig. 3.4.

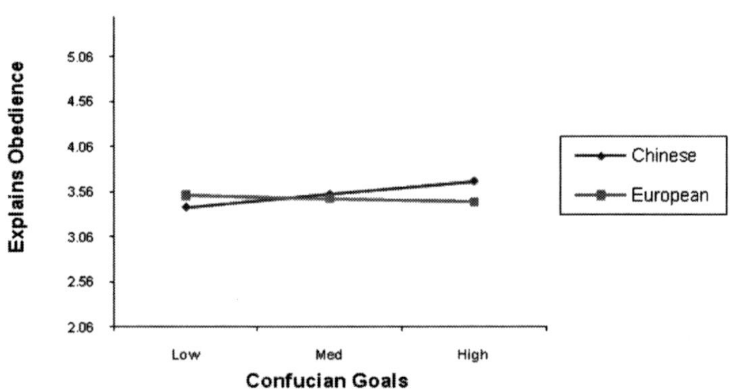

Fig. 3.4 The interactive effect of ethnicity and Confucian goals on explains obedience reported by adolescents

With parents' reports, no ethnic differences in the association between Confucian goals and Explains Obedience were found. Based on the sample as a whole, positive associations between Confucian goals and Explains Obedience were found, net of all other factors [$B = 0.24$, $SE = 0.04$, $p < 0.01$].

Adolescent & parent reports of warmth. For both adolescents' and parents' reports, no ethnic group differences were found in the associations between parental goals, Confucian or child-centered, and warmth (see Table 3.8). Thus, analyses were then conducted on the overall sample. Based on both adolescents' and parents' reports, positive associations between the *Child-centered* goals and warmth were found [$B = 0.25$, $SE = 0.09$, $p < 0.01$] and [$B = 0.20$, $SE = 0.04$, $p < 0.01$], respectively. Based on adolescents' report, though, a negative association was also found between Confucian goals and warmth [$B = -0.27$, $SE = 0.07$, $p < 0.01$].

Table 3.8 Multiple regressions of ethnicity, family characteristics, parenting goals and interaction terms for ethnicity and parenting goals on warmth

	Adolescents[a]			Parents[b]		
	B	*SE*	*Sig.*	*B*	*SE*	*Sig.*
Adolescent gender (female)	0.11	0.09	0.21	0.13	0.04	0.00
Primary caregiver (mother)	−0.01	0.12	0.95	0.04	0.06	0.52
Parent's education	−0.01	0.01	0.71	−0.01	0.01	0.16
Home ownership	0.02	0.11	0.85	0.01	0.05	0.90
Single parenthood	−0.03	0.15	0.85	0.01	0.07	0.99
Parent's income	0.03	0.04	0.38	−0.04	0.02	0.02
Confucian goals	−0.13	0.11	0.23	0.02	0.05	0.66
Child-centered goals	0.24	0.13	0.06	0.27	0.06	0.00
Ethnicity (Chinese)	−0.22	0.62	0.73	0.65	0.30	0.03
Ethnicity (Chinese) × Confucian	0.06	0.16	0.69	−0.09	0.08	0.22
Ethnicity (Chinese) × Child-centered	−0.12	0.19	0.54	−0.07	0.09	0.43

[a]$N = 563$, $R^2 = 0.08$, $F(11, 551) = 4.09$, $p < 0.01$
[b]$N = 566$, $R^2 = 0.12$, $F(11, 554) = 7.01$, $p < 0.01$

In sum, there were no ethnic group differences in the association between both subscales of behavioral control, and either Confucian or child-centered goals. However, associations were found in the sample overall such that Restricted Autonomy was negatively related to Confucian goals, and Strictness was positively related. On the other hand, ethnic differences were found in the associations involving the two components of guan, Expects Obedience and Explains Obedience, such that these aspects of guan were more positively associated with Confucian goals among Chinese Americans than European Americans. However, the third component of guan, Contingent Autonomy, was positively associated with Confucian goals for the sample overall, and ethnic differences were found only between Contingent Autonomy and Child-centered goals with this association being more positive among Chinese Americans than European Americans.

Discussion

In this investigation, we attempted to capture the cultural processes underlying parents' practices by examining how parents' beliefs influence their parental control behaviors and warmth. First, we examined whether there were ethnic group differences in the frequency levels of parenting beliefs and practices. Second, we tested the associations between parental goals and parenting practices reported by adolescents and parents. The results indicated that based on both adolescents' and parents' reports, Chinese Americans endorsed parental control behaviors and Confucian parental goals more than European Americans. However, in looking at the types of control endorsed most by the Chinese Americans, two components of guan, Contingent Autonomy and Explains Obedience, were endorsed or practiced to a greater extent than behavioral control. In the primary analyses that examined the relations among parenting goals and control practices, parental control was more strongly related to Confucian goals among Chinese American immigrants than European Americans. In some cases, though, both Confucian and Child-centered goals influenced the parental control (i.e., Contingent Autonomy) of immigrant Chinese American parents. This study provides an empirical demonstration of the cultural processes that influence parental practices through the construct of parental goals (i.e., Confucian and Child-centered); little prior research has attempted to directly assess cultural processes. Our findings support those of others who have pointed to the importance of cultural "meanings" attributed to parenting practices (Kagitcibaasi, 1996; Super & Harkness, 1986).

A limitation of the study was the low-scale reliabilities for the *parents*' reports of their practices, and this was found among both the Chinese Americans and European Americans. This is striking in that this study relied upon an established, highly used measure for parental practices (the subscales from the CRPBI). Although there were slight differences in the response formats for adolescents (from 1 = Not at all like to 5 = A lot like) and parents (from 1 = Strongly disagree to 5 = Strongly agree), the response scale for parents does not appear to be any more problematic than that for adolescents. The fact that these low-scale consistencies were mostly isolated to parents' reports may reflect the greater potential diversity in this group and its concomitant challenges in establishing measurement consistency. That is, all the Chinese American parents in this study were first-generation immigrants, so it may have been particularly challenging to establish measurement consistency for them relative to all others. In any case, the low-scale reliabilities for parents may reflect potential differences in measurement properties between adolescents and parents that are compounded further when one of the comparison groups is entirely comprised of immigrants.

In spite of the limitations of the measures, the findings that there are ethnic differences in levels of parenting practices support the argument that there are cultural distinctions in parenting. This study also documents the potentially different interpretations that adolescents may have of parenting compared to their parents, and highlights the need for capturing both perspectives. This may be particularly necessary when studying immigrant families, who may have even more generational differences than those found among European Americans. Indeed, this study has shown that there was less association between adolescents' and parents' reports among the Chinese Americans than the European Americans. In the sections below we summarize our results and their implications, focusing first on parents' beliefs and practices, and then on the interplay between parents' and adolescents' perspectives on parenting.

Associations Between Parents' Beliefs or Goals and Their Practices

Parenting goals that emphasize Confucian values were more important and child-centered values less important for immigrant Chinese Americans than European Americans, as predicted. This is consistent with Chao's (1995, 1996) studies of mothers of children in preschool that found that the Chinese Americans endorsed Confucian themes emphasizing education and making sacrifices for the child's education, a more direct intervention approach to the child's schooling and learning, and a belief that they can play a significant role in their children's school success. On the other hand, with their parenting beliefs, the European American mothers were primarily concerned about too much emphasis on academics, and the need for a less directive approach to learning that builds the child's self-esteem.

We found several differences across ethnic groups in the relations between parental goals and practices. Specifically, two subscales of guan (i.e., Expects Obedience and Explains Obedience) were more strongly related to parental goals emphasizing Confucian values for Chinese Americans than European Americans. These associations were found with both adolescent and parent reports with one exception (for parent reports, no ethnic differences in the association between Confucian goals and Explains Obedience were found, as these associations were positive for all parents). These results were consistent with predictions, and demonstrate the role of guan in shaping parenting beliefs and practices. However, contrary to predictions, the Contingent Autonomy subscale of guan was more positively related to Child-centered goals for Chinese American than European Americans, but only for parent reports. Also based on parent reports, the Confucian goals were positively related to Contingent Autonomy for the sample as a whole. Thus, for immigrant Chinese American parents, this component of guan is influenced by both Confucian and child-centered beliefs. These unexpected findings require further examination.

Results also revealed that for both ethnic groups there were positive associations between warmth and the child-centered goals, and negative associations between warmth and Confucian goals. Therefore, parental practices of warmth are just as highly informed by *child-centered* parental beliefs for Chinese Americans as they are for European Americans. Parents who tend to practice warmth, as measured by the Acceptance subscale of the CRPBI (defined by praising, showing his/her "love," giving care and attention, and being there for the child by listening to their problems) also tend to endorse Child-centered goals. It may be that even when they value Confucian goals, immigrant Chinese parents are adapting these goals to those that are dominant in the United States. This study has also found that among both groups of parents, the Confucian goals are related to the Child-centered goals, but this association was more than twice as strong for immigrant Chinese parents than European American parents.

We have demonstrated the centrality of parental beliefs that reflect Confucian values in motivating the parental control of immigrant Chinese Americans. In fact, in looking at the findings within immigrant Chinese Americans, Confucian goals were positively related to every type of parental control, sometimes based on *both* adolescent and parent reports. However, although ethnic group differences were found in the associations between Confucian goals and guan (two of the three subscales), ethnic group differences were not found in the associations between Confucian goals and the subscales of behavioral control, as well as warmth. Thus, although the Confucian goals do not appear to inform the behavioral control and warmth of immigrant Chinese American parents any more than they do for European American parents, these goals do inform the parental control defined by guan more for Chinese immigrant families than European Americans.

Adolescents' and Parents' Perspectives

This study demonstrates, based on both adolescent and parent reports, that the strictness subscale of behavioral control, and two subscales for guan (i.e., Explains Obedience, and Expects Obedience) were more frequently endorsed among Chinese Americans than European Americans. These findings are consistent with previous studies that show more controlling parenting practices among Chinese Americans (Chao, 1994, 2005; Steinberg, Lamborn, Dornbusch, & Darling, 1992). Contrary to expectations, however, Chinese American *parents* reported higher levels of warmth than European American parents, whereas Chinese American *adolescents* reported lower levels of warmth for their parents than European American adolescents did. Also, Chinese American parents reported less Restricted Autonomy (one of two subscales of behavioral control) than European American parents, whereas Chinese American *adolescents* reported slightly higher levels than did European American adolescents. Thus, with both Restricted Autonomy and warmth, adolescents' reports of parenting were more consistent with the hypotheses than parents' reports. It may be that immigrant Chinese parents are trying to appear more like European Americans, or the culture of the majority, by reporting more autonomy granting and warmth. On the other hand, Chinese American adolescents' expectations for their parents, in light of their understanding of dominant cultural images of parenting, may lead them to both expect and report less warmth and more restricted autonomy compared to their European American peers (Wu & Chao, 2005).

Additionally, consistent with expectations, greater discrepancies between adolescents' and parents' reports of parental practices were more consistently found for Chinese Americans than European Americans. Also, parents and adolescents ratings were more highly correlated among the European Americans, and in some cases twice as highly correlated, than among the Chinese Americans. These results point to the importance of work that examines the contextualized meanings of parenting practices and behaviors. Among immigrant families, differences between family members in reports of parenting or family practices in general may be heightened, due to potential differences in acculturation. These differences in acculturation extend beyond the typical generational gaps that all families experience (Wu & Chao, 2005).

As we have noted, immigrant Chinese parents more frequently endorsed two components of guan (Explains Obedience and Contingent Autonomy) than behavioral control; Chinese American adolescents also reported higher levels of Explains Obedience than the Strictness component of behavioral control. However, contrary to expectations immigrant Chinese parents relied less on the third component of guan, Expects Obedience, than behavioral control. The features of guan that include telling and continually reminding youth of their expectations are not something that immigrant Chinese parents endorse, and thus require further examination. Interestingly though, Chinese American adolescents report much higher levels of this aspect of guan than their parents do. Chinese American adolescents were also similar to their European American counterparts in reporting higher levels of Restricted Autonomy than both Expects Obedience and Contingent Autonomy; among both European American adolescents and parents Restricted Autonomy was the only component of behavioral control rated higher than guan.

In summary, these results offer a comprehensive and explicit way of conceptualizing and measuring the cultural processes underlying parenting. The results extend the findings of the second chapter, which showed distinctive differences in parenting measures as reported by Chinese American adolescents in a large national study. The findings in this chapter suggest a cultural, specifically Confucian underpinning of expectations and understandings of parent behavior in Chinese American families; the generational discrepancies between Chinese American parents and adolescents point to the importance of the immigration experience for parent-adolescent relationships.

References

Bierman, K. L. (1983). Cognitive development and clinical interview with children. In B. B. Lahey & A. E. Kazdin (Eds.), *Advances in clinical child psychology* (Vol. 6, pp. 217–250). New York: Plenum.

Blyth, D. A. (1992). Mapping the social world of adolescents: Issues, techniques and problems. In F. Refica (Ed.), *Social cognitive development in context* (pp. 240–272). New York: Guilford Press.

Boocock, S. S. (1991). Childhood and childcare in Japan and the United States: A comparative analysis. In P. A. Adler & P. Adler (Series Eds.) & N. Mandell (Vol. Ed.), *Sociological studies of child development: Vol. 4. Perspectives on and of children* (pp. 51–88). Greenwich, CT: Jai Press Inc.

Broffenbrenner, U. (1977). Toward an experimental ecology of human development. *American Psychologist*, *32*, 513–531.

Chao, R. K. (1994). Beyond parental control and authoritarian parenting style: Understanding Chinese parenting through the cultural notion of training. *Child Development, 65*, 1111–1119.

Chao, R. K. (1995). Chinese and European American cultural models of the self reflected in mothers' childrearing beliefs. *Ethos, 23*, 328–354.

Chao, R. K. (1996). Chinese and European American mothers' beliefs about the role of parenting in children's school success. *Journal of Cross-Cultural Psychology, 27*, 403–423.

Chao, R. K. (2000a). Cultural explanations for the role of parenting in the school success of Asian American children. In R. Taylor & M. Wang (Eds.), *Resilience across contexts: Family, work, culture, and community*. Hillsdale, NJ: Lawrence Erlbaum Press.

Chao, R. K. (2000b). The parenting of immigrant Chinese American and European American mothers: Relations between parenting styles, socialization goals, and parental practices. *Journal of Applied Developmental Psychology, 21*, 233–248.

Chao, R. K. (2001). Extending research on the consequences of parenting style for Chinese Americans and European Americans. *Child Development, 72*, 1832–1843.

Chao, R. K. (2005). *The importance of Guan in describing the parental control of immigrant Chinese American*. Unpublished manuscript, University of California at Riverside.

Chao, R. K., & Tran, P. (2000). *Effect of parental control and warmth across Chinese American-, Mexican-, and European American-American adolescents*. Unpublished manuscript, University of California at Riverside.

Chao, R. K., & Wu, C. (2001). *Guan parenting behaviors*. Unpublished assessment instrument, University of California at Riverside.

Chen, S.-J. (1996). Positive childishness: Images of childhood in Japan. In C. P. Hwang, M. E. Lamb, & I. E. Sigel (Eds.), *Images of childhood* (pp. 113–128). Mahwah, NJ: Lawrence Erlbaum Associates.

Gallimore, R., Goldenberg, C. N., & Weisner, T. S. (1993). The social construction and subjective reality of activity settings: Implications for community psychology. *American Journal of Community Psychology, 21*, 537–559.

Goodnow, J. J., & Collins, W. A. (1990). *Development according to parents: The nature, sources and consequences of parents' ideas*. East Sussex, UK: Laurence Erlbaum Associates Ltd.

Guadagnoli, E., & Velicer, W. (1988). Relation of sample size to the stability of component patterns. *Psychological Bulletin, 103*, 265–275.

Kagitcibaasi, C. (1996). *Family and human development across cultures*. Mahwah, NJ: Erlbaum.

Kojima, H. (1986). Japanese concepts of child development from the mid-17th century to the mid-19th century. *International Journal of Behavioral Development, 9*, 315–329

McGillicuddy-DeLisi, A. V., De Lisi, R., Flaugher, J., & Sigel, I. E. (1987). Familial influences on planning. In S. L. Friedman & E. K. Scholnick (Eds.), *Blueprints for thinking: The role of planning in cognitive development* (pp. 395–427). Cambridge, England: Cambridge University Press.

Schaefer, E. S. (1965). Children's reports of parental behavior: An inventory. *Child Development, 36*(2), 413–424.

Schludermann, E. H., & Schludermann, S. M. (1988). *Children's report on parent behavior* (CRPBI-108, CRPBI-30 for children and older adolescents, Technical Report). Winnipeg, MB, Canada: University of Manitoba.

Sigel, I. E., McGillicudy-DeLisi, A. V., & Goodnow, J. J. (1992). *Parental belief systems: The psychological consequences for children*. Hillsdale, NJ: Lawrence Erlbaum

Steinberg, L., Lamborn, S. D., Dornbusch, S. M., & Darling, N. (1992). Impact of parenting practices on adolescent achievement: Authoritative parenting, school involvement, and encouragement to succeed. *Child Development, 63*, 1266–1281.

Super, C. M., & Harkness, S. (1986). The developmental niche: A conceptualization at the interface of child and culture. *International Journal of Behavioral Development, 9*, 545–569.

Wu, C. X., & Chao, R. K. (2005). Intergenerational cultural conflicts for Chinese American youth with immigrant parents: Norms of parental warmth and the consequences. *International Journal of Behavioral Development, 29*, 516–523.

Chapter 4
Parental Sacrifice and Acceptance as Distinct Dimensions of Parental Support Among Chinese and Filipino American Adolescents

Ruth K. Chao and Kevin F. Kaeochinda

The prior chapter focused on the cultural underpinnings of parenting through a comparative study of Chinese American and European American parents and adolescents. The notable cultural differences had to do with the construct of parental control: measures of *guan* were more strongly linked to parental goals based in Confucian values for Chinese American than European American parents. Parental practices of warmth, by contrast, were equally informed by culturally based parenting beliefs for both groups. However, parental support historically has been conceptualized largely in terms of warmth and acceptance, yet this lens on parental support may ignore other culturally meaningful dimensions of parenting (Chao, 1994). This chapter offers a new approach for understanding parental support through incorporating a distinct dimension in addition to parental warmth: parental sacrifice.

Parental support is a central construct in research on parenting and parent-adolescent relationships, yet there is little research that examines youths' interpretation and understanding of parental support. Further, although there is reason to believe that such understandings of parental support may vary culturally, there is little work that examines such cultural variability across or within ethnic groups. Many studies have shown that parental support is beneficial for youth both cross-nationally and among some immigrant groups in the United States, but few have examined parental support in different Asian American ethnic subgroups (e.g., Chinese and Filipino Americans). Furthermore, since many measures of parental practices, including parental support, were originally created for middle class, European Americans (Julian, McHenry, & McKelvey, 1994), there is little understanding of how specific Asian immigrant groups endorse and assess these parent practices. Parental sacrifice has been suggested as a central feature of parenting in Asian culture (Chao, 1994), yet this dimension of parenting has not been conceptualized in relation to parental support in the existing research literature. This study aims to examine the construct of parental support, arguing that for Asian

R.K. Chao (✉)
University of California, Riverside, CA, USA
e-mail: ruth.chao@ucr.edu

S.T. Russell et al. (eds.), *Asian American Parenting and Parent-Adolescent Relationships*, Advancing Responsible Adolescent Development,
DOI 10.1007/978-1-4419-5728-3_4,

immigrant families in the United States it consists of two facets: parental acceptance and parental sacrifice.

This study is designed to show that parental sacrifice is part of a broader construct of parental support that is distinct from parental acceptance. That is, our goal is to show that parental sacrifice is a distinct facet of parental support that is reflective of the cultural features and cultural frames of reference of Asian immigrants (Chao, 1994; Lansford et al., 2005). In this study, we examined the meaning of parental support based on adolescents' response to survey measures of their perception of parental acceptance and sacrifice. Ultimately, the aim of this study is to better understand and improve the psychometric properties of parental support (acceptance and sacrifice) for two Asian ethnic subgroups (Chinese and Filipino Americans). The study examines measurement equivalence to ascertain the extent to which Chinese and Filipino American adolescents interpret parental support in similar or unique ways.

Although there may be common features for defining and expressing parental support among Asian Americans, studies have rarely examined differences in the psychometric properties of parental support measures across Asian American ethnic groups. Ethnic differences among Asian Americans have largely been ignored in previous research in that most studies tend to pool Asian Americans into a single, homogenous group.

For this study our approach is to investigate the measurement equivalence of parental support for two distinct Asian American ethnic groups, Chinese and Filipinos. Between these two distinct ethnic groups there may be differences in the way each group conceptualizes and endorses parental support, resulting in invariance in the measurement of parental support (Crockett, Randall, Shen, Russell, & Driscoll, 2005; Hui & Triandis, 1985). The differences in conceptualization of parenting that we hypothesize may be rooted in the distinct cultural histories of these ethnic groups. For example, Blair and Qian (1998) suggested that Filipino American adolescents, as compared to Chinese Americans, differed considerably with respect to language usage (e.g., speaking native language at home), educational aspirations, and attitudes towards Western ideologies. Specifically, Filipino families tend to use English at home while their Chinese peers more often speak their native language at home. The use of English at home may be more facilitative for adopting Western ideologies (Blair & Qian, 1998), including ideologies related to family relationships and parenting. Furthermore, whereas East Asian countries like China have been influenced by unifying cultural principles or philosophies such as those of Confucius and Buddhism (Chao, 1994, 1995), Filipinos have not. Specifically, Filipino cultural principles are harder to define due to their unique socio-cultural history of colonization by Spain, Great Britain, Japan, and the United States, varying dialects among the islands, and unique economic subsystems (Bacho, 1997; Espiritu, 1995; Kitano & Daniels, 1995).

Parental Acceptance (Warmth)

Previous research has shown that high levels of perceived parental acceptance are related to psychological and behavioral adjustment in children and adolescents

(Rohner, Khaleque, & Cournoyer, 2005; Schaefer, 1965b). Many of these studies have specifically relied on the parental acceptance subscale of the Child's Report of Parental Behavior Inventory(CRPBI) (Schaefer, 1959, 1965a, 1965b; Schludermann & Schludermann, 1970, 1983). This subscale of parental acceptance includes items for capturing parents' concern and involvement (e.g., "Gives me a lot of care and attention"), as well as warmth and responsiveness (e.g., "Believes in showing her/his love for me").

Rohner (1960, 1975) has also conducted a number of cross-cultural studies of parental support based on his Parental Acceptance-Rejection Theory (PARTheory), and the development of the Parental Acceptance-Rejection Questionnaire (PARQ) (Rohner et al., 2005). PARTheory suggests a bipolar dimension of rejection and acceptance by the caregiver with feelings of warmth and acceptance on one end, and rejection and withdrawal on the other. Rohner and colleagues (2005) have noted that youth perceptions of the amount of acceptance and warmth by a caregiver explained up to 26% of the variability of youths' psychological adjustment. In addition, Rohner and colleagues have demonstrated the cross-cultural significance of his measure of parental acceptance: greater warmth or feelings of acceptance have been found to be associated with outcomes like emotional stability for children from a number of societies including, the United States, China, India, Finland, and Turkey (Rohner et al., 2005). However, these researchers have also emphasized possible cultural-specific components to children's overall perception of this acceptance in that "...the key concepts of perceived acceptance and rejection are defined in terms of the interpretations that children and adults make of major caregivers' behaviors" (p. 301). In other words, the actual parenting behaviors that constitute children's feelings of acceptance from parents are specific to their culture, or to how acceptance is conveyed by parents. For example, Rohner provides an observation of a 9-year-old Bengali child who reported the love and acceptance she felt from her mother by the mother's simple act of peeling and removing seeds from an orange (Parmar & Rohner, 2008).

These cultural features of parental acceptance may be part of a broader concept that some have referred to as parental support. Parental support consists of parenting behaviors that foster closeness between parent and child, including feelings that parents are involved and responsive to their children, as defined above for parental acceptance. However, Grotevant (1987) suggests that the context in which this occurs is important, and that cultural features of parental acceptance are part of a broader construct of parental support. Specifically, societal norms, cultural practices, and the influence of family values affect the way parents and their children interpret support. An additional cultural feature of parental acceptance or, broadly parental support, for many Asian immigrant families would include parental sacrifice.

Parental Sacrifice

For Asian immigrant families in the United States, the migration experience itself may often constitute some sacrifice on the part of parents, such as leaving higher paying jobs for better opportunities in the United States, including educational opportunities and upward mobility for their children (Bullock & Waugh, 2005; Fuligni & Yoshikawa, 2002). Such sacrifices further reinforce additional investments that parents make in order to ensure their children will take advantage of these opportunities. One of the primary ways that Asian immigrant parents ensure their children's welfare is by providing not only instrumental support, continually ensuring their daily needs are met, but also providing parental involvement and resources they need to succeed in school (Chao & Tseng, 2002; Hyman, Vu, & Beiser, 2001; Pyke, 2000).

In most studies that examine the cultural processes of parenting for Asian immigrant families there has been little focus on youths' perceptions of the contributions parents make to their success. Most previous research on cultural features of their parenting and family socialization has tended to focus on youths' duty or obligation to their families, and/or their obedience or respect for parents in the larger context of filial piety. Yet prior studies have not examined the parenting processes that are most influential in fostering these feelings of obligation, obedience, and respect in children. In fact, previous research has shown that Asian American adolescents have greater feelings of obligation and adherence to their family when compared to their European American peers (Hardway & Fuligni, 2006). Asian American adolescents are expected to take care of siblings and household chores, and provide primary care for their aging parents (Chen, Bond, & Tang, 2007). Specifically, previous research has shown that even busy adults are more likely to provide at-home care (e.g., home care workers) for their aging parents than to use other settings such as retirement homes (Cheung, Kwan, & Ng, 2006; Lan, 2002).

Confucian notions of family life provide the foundation for tenets of children's obligation and obedience to, as well as respect for, their parents. Specifically, the roles of children and parents are hierarchically defined through the benevolence of parents in caring for their children and through the reciprocation of the children to the parents to carry out their parents' wishes and expectations (Chao, 1994; Kim & Rohner, 2002; Park & Chelsa, 2007). This concept is related to a broader concept of filial piety. The concept of filial piety, and its features of obedience, honor, and respect towards parents, has helped to more clearly define children's obligatory roles to their parents (Chao & Tseng, 2002). However, studies have not explicitly examined how such a sense of obligation and respect in children is fostered by parents, or the roles that parents play in incurring such obligation, responsibility, and respect for their parents.

In order to understand the obligatory role that children adopt for their parents, Wu (2007) has argued that this role evolves from the reciprocal nature of parent-child relationships. She has described this reciprocity through the Chinese notion of *qin* (Wu, 2007). Specifically, qin can be understood as the bonds created between adolescent and parent through the parent's investment in the adolescent's welfare. Such parental investment includes giving whatever resources parents can bear for the betterment of their children. This investment by parents is manifested through their continual, instrumental support rather than through verbal expressions (e.g., "I love you") or demonstrations of physical affection that is common in Western style parenting such as the United States (Chao & Tseng, 2002). Although this facet of Asian parents' behaviors may be interpreted as less warm from a Western point of view, Asian children and adolescents may perceive and understand this sacrifice from parents as part of how their parents love and care for them.

Current Study

In this study, we investigate the factor structure and cross-ethnic item-level measurement equivalence of parental support measures (acceptance and sacrifice). We show that, among two Asian American ethnic groups, parental support consists of two related but distinct factors of parental acceptance and parental sacrifice: the latter reflects the cultural component of parental support. Second, we examine measurement equivalence of parental acceptance and sacrifice across two ethnic groups of Asian American youth from immigrant families, Chinese and Filipinos, to gain a better understanding of how Chinese American and Filipino American adolescents define and understand parental support. Although similar to the second chapter in this volume in our focus on the equivalence of measures across ethnic subgroups, our approach differs in that, rather than focus on establishing invariance for existing measures between ethnic groups, our goal is to develop of a new measure of parental sacrifice.

Specifically, the purpose of this study is to describe the measurement structure and measurement equivalence of a set of parental support items administered to Chinese- and Filipino-American adolescents. Using an approach suggested by Muthén (1984), we examine the dimensionality of parental support scales via exploratory and confirmatory factor analysis models, and measurement equivalence, across Filipino and Chinese adolescents by estimating confirmatory factor analysis models with covariates (i.e., multiple indicator, multiple cause structural equation models) and multiple-group confirmatory factor analysis models.

The survey questions were developed based on conceptual and cultural understandings of acceptance (Schludermann & Schludermann, 1988) and sacrifice (Chao, 1994, 2001a, 2001b). In the analyses of the structural and measurement properties of parental support, we expect that a two-factor structure of acceptance and sacrifice will fit the data better than a one-factor structure of support. However, both factors will be highly correlated indicating that they are both components of the broader notion of parental support.

First, analyses were conducted to test whether the factor structure (structural solution) of parental support is consistent with our underlying conceptual model that parental acceptance and sacrifice are two distinct aspects (or factors). Exploratory factor analysis (EFA) models were estimated comparing the model fit of a one-factor solution, a two-factor solution, and also a possible three-factor solution. The latter was also included to determine whether acceptance or sacrifice would further separate into sub-domains in additional factors. We ran these same analyses on the sample as a whole, and then separately for Chinese and Filipino Americans. The results of the EFA models were used as a starting point for a series of CFA models.

Based on results of the EFAs, the model fit of a one-, two-, and three-factor structure was then compared through a series of CFAs for the whole sample, and for Chinese and Filipinos separately. A combination of criteria was used to determine the number of factors to retain in the EFAs, i.e., scree plots and the number of eigenvalues greater than 1, conceptual clarity, simplicity (parsimonious model), and models with item loadings at least 0.60 with no cross-loadings.

Once the factor structure was determined, further examinations of measurement invariance were conducted with a focus on both item intercepts and factor loadings. However, our approach for these examinations was at the specific item level, in addition to the global level (i.e., looking at overall model fit). That is, because our measure is based on a specific conceptual or theoretical model, we sought to look at invariance for specific items by relying on modification indices of each item (representing each construct or latent factor). Once the specific items that needed to be freed were determined (through examination of intercepts or factors loadings), we tested a model with these items freed across ethnic groups to one in which all items were constrained to be equal. To determine whether there are differences in model fit between the base (constrained) model and unconstrained model (in which intercepts and/or factor loadings are freed) we relied on the comparative fit index (CFI), Tucker-Lewis Index (TLI), and root mean square error of approximation (RMSEA).[1]

Finally, reliability and validity were assessed for parental acceptance and parental sacrifice. Internal consistency estimates of reliability of the derived scales were calculated using Cronbach's alpha for each ethnic group and for the whole sample. Nunnaly's (1978) criterion of 0.70 was used as the cutoff for determining acceptable internal consistency reliability.

Method

Participants

The total sample consisted of 941 ninth graders from eight different high schools in the greater Los Angeles area, including 598 Chinese Americans (198 first generation and 400 second generation) and 343 Filipino Americans (117 first generation and 226 second generation) drawn from a larger longitudinal data set.

There were a total of 478 males (286 Chinese and 192 Filipinos) and 458 females (308 Chinese and 150 Filipinos) with 5 adolescents that did not report their gender. Of the females, 155 were first generation and 303 were second generation; of the

[1] Chapter 2 provides a fuller description of the use of these indices in testing model fit. We also checked whether there was a significant change in X^2(X^2 difference test) between the constrained model and the model when intercepts or loadings were freed. However, as this test is sensitive to sample size, with large sample sizes often resulting in significant differences, we did not rely on this test.

males 159 were first generation and 319 were second generation. The overall mean age for first-generation and second-generation Asian Americans was 14.83 (*SD* = 0.70) and 14.63 (*SD* = 0.53) years, respectively. Among the Chinese Americans, the mean age of mother's immigration was 28.25 (*SD* = 8.92) and the mean age of father's immigration was 30.31 (*SD* = 9.94). Among the Filipino Americans, the mean age of mother's immigration was 27.73 (*SD* = 10.03) and the mean age of father's immigration was 29.13 (*SD* = 10.33).

Measures and Procedures

Consent. Parental consent was obtained prior to students' participation in the study. Consent forms were mailed beforehand to parents of adolescents to request their children's participation. Parents were required to send back the consent forms only if they did *not* wish their child to participate in this study. All parents received copies of consent letters in English, Chinese, and Korean, along with a postage-paid, self-addressed envelope. Adolescents were also provided with an assent statement on the cover page of their survey. Adolescents completed these paper-and-pencil surveys, consisting of the following measures, during one of their class periods.

Parental acceptance. Parental acceptance was measured through the acceptance-rejection scale of the Children's Report on Parent Behavior Inventory (CRPBI-30) (Schaefer, 1965a, 1965b) adapted by Schludermann and Schludermann (1988) for adolescents (Youth Self Report). The scale includes 10 items involving parental responsiveness and involvement. See Table 4.1 for the list of items. Responses to the items were measured on a five-point Likert-type scale from 1 = "not at all like" to 5 = "a lot like."

Table 4.1 Description of parental support measures (parental acceptance and parental sacrifice)

Construct	Item wording
Parental acceptance	Enjoys doing things with me
	Gives me a lot of care and attention
	Praises me often
	Is easy to talk to
	Makes me feel like the most important person in her/his life
	Is able to make me feel better when I am upset
	Makes me feel better after talking over my worries with her/him
	Smiles at me very often
	Believes in showing her/his love for me
	Cheers me up when I am sad
Parental sacrifice	My parents has made many sacrifices to give me a better life
	My parents work hard to assure that I have the best opportunities
	My parents have really tried hard to give me opportunities that they did not have
	My parents has faced great challenges to get where s/he is
	I am grateful to my parent for everything s/he has tried to do for me
	I feel I owe a lot to my parent for everything s/he has tried to do for me

Parental sacrifice. Parental sacrifice was measured through six items developed for a larger study on parenting of Asian immigrants. These items were designed to capture two components: parents' sacrifice and hard work for assuring their children have a better life and children's gratitude and recognition of parental sacrifice. See Table 4.1 for the list of items. Responses to the items were measured on a five-point Likert-type scale from: 1 = "strongly disagree" to 5 = "strongly agree."

Results

Demographic characteristics of the analytic sample by ethnic group (Chinese and Filipinos) are provided in Table 4.2. Both ethnic subsamples included roughly equal numbers of boys and girls. Chinese Americans were younger on average than their Filipino American peers. Chinese Americans reported their mothers as their primary caregiver more often than their Filipino American peers.

Table 4.2 Means (standard errors) or percentages for demographic variables and parental support (acceptance and sacrifice) by ethnic group (Chinese and Filipino)

	Chinese $N = 598$	Filipino $N = 343$	Differences across groups
Single parent status	0.11 (0.32)	0.10 (0.29)	n.s.
Gender (female)	0.52 (0.50)	0.44 (0.50)	n.s.
Child's age	14.12 (0.37)	14.19 (0.40)	C < F
Mother's education	8.32 (13.18)	9.16 (14.56)	n.s.
Father's education	6.85 (1.53)	6.33 (1.76)	n.s.
Age of immigration (mother)	28.25 (8.92)	27.73 (10.03)	n.s.
Age of immigration (father)	30.31 (9.94)	29.13 (10.33)	n.s.
Primary caregiver (mother)	0.84 (0.37)	0.75 (0.43)	F < C

Note: C = All Chinese, F = All Filipino; the findings for the across-group differences were based on an alpha level of 0.05, n.s. = not significant; Gender (Female) was encoded with 1 = Female and 0 = Male.

Structural Analyses of Parental Support

The first step in our series of analyses included EFAs and CFAs that were conducted for determining whether a two-factor structure, reflecting the two dimensions of acceptance and sacrifice, best fits the data compared to a one-factor or three-factor structure. To derive estimates for the EFA and CFA models, Muthén and Muthén's (2008) Mplus statistical modeling program was used. Because all the items used to measure parental support are categorical, Muthén's (1984) approach to exploratory and confirmatory factor analysis with categorical indicators was used. Since these models involve a categorical dependent variable that is influenced by and influences either another observed dependent variable or latent variable, theta parameterization as suggested by Muthén and Muthén (2008) was used to examine the residual variances. The number of factors was examined using Promax oblique rotation that allowed the items to correlate because we hypothesized that parental acceptance and parental sacrifice would be related but distinct constructs.

Based on the whole sample overall, the scree plot of eigenvalues (i.e., the number of eigenvalues greater than 1) indicated possible one- or two-factor structure solutions. For the whole sample ($N = 941$), in the one-factor structure model, most of the items had loadings greater than 0.80 with the exception of one item loading at 0.64. In the two-factor structure model, there were no items that loaded on more than one factor, and all items loaded on each primary factor at 0.65 or above. However, in the three-factor model, 2 of the 10 items for parental acceptance (i.e., "Is easy to talk to," and "Cheers me up when I am sad") loaded on both the first and third factors, and two additional items (i.e., "Is able to make me feel better when I am upset," and "Makes me feel better after talking over my worries with me") loaded on the third factor exclusively. All the parental sacrifice items loaded on the second factor with no double loadings on another factor.

When these same EFAs were run again for Chinese and Filipinos separately, for both groups, the scree plots with eigenvalues greater than 1 indicated possible one- and two-factor structure solutions only. We present the one- and two-factor solutions for each group in Table 4.3. For the subsample of Chinese ($N = 598$), the one-, two-, and three-factor structures, were similar to that described above for the whole or overall sample, with the three-factor structure yielding double loadings for the same two acceptance items as in the overall sample and also the same additional two items for acceptance loading on a third factor. For the subsample of Filipinos ($N = 343$), however, in the two-factor solution, we found two items of parental sacrifice ("I am grateful to my parent for everything s/he has tried to do for me" and "I feel I owe a lot to my parent for everything s/he has tried to do for me") that loaded on more than one factor. That is, the former item loaded at 0.45 on the first factor, comprising the parental acceptance items, and 0.61 on the second, and the latter item at 0.41 on the first factor and 0.67 on the second factor. All other items loaded on each primary factor exclusively at 0.60 or above. Additionally, in the three-factor model, there were four items for parental acceptance that loaded on more than one factor. These items were "Enjoys doing things with me," "Makes me feel like I am the most important person in his/her life," "Smiles at me very often," and "Believes in showing his/her love for me."

Thus, the three-factor structure seemed to exhibit the least clarity in that not only were the eigenvalues for the third factor less than 1.0, there were at least two items that loaded on more than one factor, and an additional two acceptance items that split off from the primary factor. The two-factor model appears to demonstrate the most conceptual clarity. However, because two of the parental sacrifice items loaded on more than one factor for Filipinos, the EFAs were re-run after dropping the items that double-loaded. The two-factor structure without these two items fit the data well for both ethnic groups and the overall sample in that the eigenvalues were above 1.0, and all items loaded on their primary factor at 0.64 or greater, with

Table 4.3 Factor loadings and communalities from exploratory factor analyses with promax rotation for 1 and 2 factor (acceptance and sacrifice) solutions for a measure of parental support

	Chinese			Filipino		
	1 Factor	2 Factor		1 Factor	2 Factor	
	Support	Accept	Sacrifice	Support	Accept	Sacrifice
10 acceptance/6 sacrifice items						
Enjoys doing things with me	0.795	0.704	0.100	0.899	0.670	0.254
Gives me a lot of care and attention	0.863	0.614	0.307	0.895	0.731	0.223
Praises me often	0.695	0.780	−0.074	0.609	0.488	0.126
Is easy to talk to	0.853	0.809	0.065	0.870	0.808	0.063
Makes me feel like the most important person in her/his life	0.860	0.732	0.180	0.907	0.670	0.261
Is able to make me feel better when I am upset	0.934	0.893	0.064	0.966	1.002	−0.074
Makes me feel better after talking over my worries with her/him	0.875	0.822	0.099	0.922	0.970	−0.091
Smiles at me very often	0.878	0.919	−0.058	0.913	0.758	0.171
Believes in showing her/his love for me	0.866	0.816	0.073	0.919	0.787	0.159
Cheers me up when I am sad	0.939	0.969	−0.049	0.951	1.025	−0.109
My parents has made many sacrifices to give me a better life	0.940	0.097	0.857	0.927	0.079	0.867
My parents work hard to assure that I have the best opportunities	0.960	0.096	0.896	0.967	0.181	0.844
My parents tried to give me opportunities that they did not have	0.889	−0.002	0.904	0.900	0.196	0.783
My parents has faced great challenges to get where s/he is	0.772	−0.172	0.918	0.906	−0.234	1.096
I am grateful to my parents for everything they have tried to do for me	0.984	0.257	0.806	0.976	0.485	0.576
I feel I owe a lot to my parent for everything s/he has tried to do	0.998	0.251	0.793	0.981	0.410	0.663
10 acceptance/4 sacrifice items						
Enjoys doing things with me	0.783	0.704	0.084	0.896	0.690	0.226
Gives me a lot of care and attention	0.846	0.677	0.218	0.887	0.749	0.199
Praises me often	0.685	0.741	−0.040	0.603	0.566	0.027
Is easy to talk to	0.834	0.828	0.007	0.850	0.806	0.035

Table 4.3 (continued)

	Chinese			Filipino		
	1 Factor	2 Factor		1 Factor	2 Factor	
	Support	Accept	Sacrifice	Support	Accept	Sacrifice
Makes me feel like the most important person in her/his life	0.841	0.724	0.166	0.900	0.701	0.223
Is able to make me feel better when I am upset	0.925	0.930	−0.013	0.954	0.994	−0.077
Makes me feel better after talking over my worries with her/him	0.856	0.853	0.025	0.919	0.964	−0.091
Smiles at me very often	0.857	0.873	−0.022	0.902	0.769	0.151
Believes in showing her/his love for me	0.851	0.809	0.088	0.920	0.786	0.167
Cheers me up when I am sad	0.928	0.976	−0.080	0.948	1.011	−0.091
My parents has made many sacrifices to give me a better life	0.923	0.113	0.822	0.930	0.121	0.843
My parents work hard to assure that I have the best opportunities	0.944	0.100	0.873	0.974	0.169	0.866
My parents tried to give me opportunities that they did not have	0.874	0.002	0.883	0.900	0.231	0.743
My parents has faced great challenges to get where s/he is	0.725	−0.133	0.831	0.906	−0.196	1.069
I am grateful to my parent for everything they have tried to do for me	Dropped	Dropped	Dropped	Dropped	Dropped	Dropped
I feel I owe a lot to my parent for everything s/he has tried to do	Dropped	Dropped	Dropped	Dropped	Dropped	Dropped

no double loadings. The results for the one- and three-factor structures were similar to those reported above.

Based on the findings from the EFA, we focused on just the one- and two-factor solutions, using CFA modeling analyses to compare the fit indices of each solution for each ethnic group separately and for the overall sample. Based on the combination of criteria for the model fit indices for the CFI, TLI, and RMSEA, presented in Table 4.4, we found that the two-factor structure solution fit the data best for the overall sample and for the two subsamples.

Furthermore, parental acceptance and parental sacrifice are highly correlated for both Chinese and Filipino ($r = 0.53$ for Chinese, $r = 0.63$ for Filipinos, and $r = 0.56$ for the overall sample). Thus, the correlation between the two factors of parental acceptance and parental sacrifice for both Chinese and Filipino showed that they are related but distinct constructs.

Table 4.4 General factor structure for separate ethnic group (Chinese and Filipino Americans) in confirmatory factor analyses

	df	X^2	CFI	TLI	RMSEA
Chinese Americans ($N = 598$)					
1-Factor (*support*)	77	441.91**	0.94	0.93	0.09
2-Factors (*acceptance & sacrifice*)	76	257.00**	0.97	0.97	0.07
Filipino Americans ($N = 343$)					
1-Factor (*support*)	77	274.18**	0.97	0.97	0.09
2-Factors (*acceptance & sacrifice*)	76	214.74**	0.98	0.98	0.08
Overall sample ($N = 872$)					
1-Factor (*support*)	77	568.09**	0.95	0.94	0.09
2-Factors (*acceptance & sacrifice*)	76	316.94**	0.97	0.97	0.06

**$p < 0.01$

Confirmatory Factor Analyses

The results of the EFA models and initial CFA analyses for comparing model fit of the factor structure models were then used as a starting point for a series of additional confirmatory factor analysis (CFA) models. To investigate measurement invariance, we first examined whether item intercepts differed across Chinese Americans and Filipino Americans by using MIMIC modeling—multiple indicator, multiple cause structural equation modeling—to test for differential item functioning across ethnic groups. Specifically, as explained above, we first examined whether there were any specific items that needed to be freed based on modification indices ($\chi^2 > 3.84$) and standardized expected parameter change (> 0.25). Then we compared the fit indices of a base model in which we constrained all item intercepts to be equal across groups to a model in which intercepts for the specific items identified above were allowed to be different for Chinese and Filipino adolescents.

In looking at the indicator intercepts in the MIMIC modeling approach, results indicated that the intercept for one acceptance item—"believes in showing his/her love for me"—was almost 25% of a standard deviation unit higher for Filipino Americans than Chinese Americans. The intercept for one sacrifice item—"my parent has really tried hard to give me opportunities that s/he did not have"—was over 40% of a standard deviation unit lower for Filipino Americans than Chinese Americans. Specifically, these results indicate that for a given level of parental acceptance, Filipino American adolescents report 25% of a standard deviation higher than Chinese American adolescents on "believes in showing his/her love for me". Similarly, for a given level on the parental sacrifice items, Filipino American adolescents score 40% of a standard deviation lower on reports on "my parent has really tried hard to give me opportunities that s/he did not have". Thus, it would appear that a given score on these two items does not mean the same thing for Filipino American and Chinese American adolescents. Based on the test of chi-square differences, model fit improved when intercepts were allowed to differ on these items than when they were constrained to be equal across ethnic groups [$\Delta X^2(2) = 18.41$, $p < 0.00$]. However, comparative fit indices (CFI), Tucker-Lewis Index (TLI), and root mean square error of approximation (RMSEA) showed very little improvement in model fit when intercepts were freed [CFI = 0.98, TLI = 0.97, RMSEA = 0.06] compared to when they were constrained to be equal across groups [CFI = 0.97, TLI = 0.97, RMSEA = 0.06]. We therefore have concluded that the measurement intercept differences identified above are not substantial enough to conclude that the items function differently across the two groups.

We examined another facet of measurement invariance, whether the factor loadings differed between the groups. In order to examine possible differences in factor loadings, we used the multiple-group approach to CFA using Muthén and Muthén's (2008) weighted least squares estimator. Similar to the approach we used with the MIMIC modeling for detecting measurement intercept differences, we examined modification indices and fully standardized expected factor loading differences (> 0.25) to ascertain differences in factor loadings across groups. Based on this criteria, there was one item, "often praises me," that was over 20% of a standard deviation unit lower for Filipinos compared to Chinese. Based on the test of chi-square differences, model fit improved when the factor loading for this item was allowed to differ than when factor loadings for all items were constrained to be equal across ethnic groups [$\Delta X^2(1) = 19.24$, $p < 0.00$]. However, comparative fit indices (CFI), Tucker-Lewis Index (TLI), and root mean square error of approximation (RMSEA) showed very little improvement in model fit when intercepts were freed [CFI = 0.98, TLI = 0.98, RMSEA = 0.07] compared to when they were constrained to be equal across groups [CFI = 0.97, TLI = 0.98, RMSEA = 0.07].

In summary, because the model fit indices were not notably different in models in which selected intercepts and loadings were *and* were not constrained to be the same for Chinese and Filipino adolescents, we concluded that there is not substantively meaningful measurement invariance involving item intercepts or factor loadings for these two groups. However, in the initial analyses (EFA) for determining similar factor structures, two (out of six) parental sacrifice items were problematic for Filipinos in that they loaded on more than one factor. Thus, in examining the reliabilities of the constructs or scales for parental acceptance and sacrifice, all 10 items comprised the parental acceptance scale, whereas only four of the original six items were retained for the parental sacrifice scale.

Reliability Analyses

Scale scores were then created for each set of items by computing the mean of the items for each set. For the parental acceptance scale, the items had excellent internal consistencies (Cronbach's alphas) with 0.85 for the whole sample (0.85 and 0.86 for the ethnic groups). The parental sacrifice scales also had excellent internal consistencies with 0.85 for the whole sample (0.84 and 0.88 for the ethnic groups). Finally, we calculated the average score on each scale for each ethnic group. We found no significant differences in the mean levels of parental acceptance (Chinese=3.37; Filipino=3.46) or parental sacrifice (Chinese=4.39Filipino=4.45) between the two groups.

Discussion

This study provided an initial understanding of the cultural meaning of parental support for Asian American youth, specifically the interpretations these youths make of the acceptance and sacrifices they receive from their parents. Based on conceptual and cultural understanding of the support provided by parents for Asian American youths, this study first demonstrated that parental acceptance and sacrifice were similar but distinct factors and that both are part of a larger construct of parental support. Then, this study investigated whether these measures of parental support work equally well for Chinese and Filipino American youth. The larger picture is that Chinese and Filipino American youth may have similar cultural understandings or perspectives of parental acceptance and sacrifice in that the measures of these constructs work equally well between Chinese and Filipinos.

As predicted, results showed that Chinese and Filipino Americans endorsed a two-factor structure of parental support rather than a single-factor structure of support. In other words, Chinese and Filipino Americans seem to incorporate a cultural component in their understanding or meaning system of parental support that extends beyond parental acceptance to that of parental sacrifice. Consistent with previous research, acceptance for Asian immigrant parents is manifested through their continual, instrumental support rather than through verbal expressions (i.e., "I love you") or demonstrations of support that are common among European Americans (Chao & Tseng, 2002), and children may come to understand these parenting behaviors as part of how their parents convey their love and acceptance (Chao, 2001a; Wu, 2007).

In the exploratory examinations for whether our measures work equally well across ethnic groups, we found that the measures for both parental acceptance and sacrifice work equally well for Chinese and Filipinos. Moreover, we tested for such equivalence on a more stringent level: we examined at the item level how *any* item, and not all items together as a totality, work for one group compared to another. Our results provide strong evidence for equivalence of measures. Thus, we conclude that this measure is applicable for both Chinese and Filipino American youth. Moreover, possible cultural differences in meaning or understanding of parental acceptance and sacrifice between these ethnic groups of Asian American youth are not evident with the measure tested in this study.

However, the evidence for measurement invariance was primarily based on item intercepts and loadings. In the initial analyses (EFAs) for determining similar factor structures we found that some of the items for parental sacrifice overlap with or share some commonalities in meaning with parental acceptance among Filipino American youth. For Filipino Americans the items "I am grateful to my parent for everything s/he has tried to do for me" and "I feel I owe a lot to my parent for everything s/he has tried to do for me" loaded on both factors of parental acceptance and parental sacrifice. The items above seem to describe a sense of gratitude or debt to parents for their sacrifices. Perhaps for Filipino American youth feelings of gratitude or indebtedness are more consistent with or dependent upon feeling accepted by parents. As there was no evidence of overlap (double loadings) involving any parental sacrifice items for Chinese American youth, their understanding of parental sacrifice may be different or less ambiguous than that of Filipino American youth.

Some caution is in order regarding the initial findings reported in this study. One limitation of the study was the fact that all surveys were administered in English. Thus, more recent immigrants who are not as fluent in English may not be represented in the study sample due to inability to complete the survey forms. Because the vast majority of Filipino immigrant youth are fairly fluent in English, and because schools in the Philippines are conducted in English, the Chinese immigrant youth would likely be more under-represented in the study sample than Filipino immigrant youth. This lack of representation may result in differences between Chinese Americans and Filipino Americans that were not detected in the current study.

These findings underscore the need for culturally sensitive measures for Asian immigrant families and adolescents. In understanding the parental support of Asian immigrants it is important to incorporate cultural features of their support that they do not necessarily share with other groups, including European Americans, as well as those that they do share with these other groups. The measures examined in this study incorporate both similarities and differences. The additional cultural features of parental sacrifice are also critical for being able to more fully capture the parental support of Asian immigrants. Although developmentally adolescents need the support of their parents, it is often unclear how adolescents interpret the sacrifices that their parents make for them. Moreover, this process may differ for Asian immigrant families compared to those families with both parents and children who are born in the United States. Asian immigrants may feel that parental sacrifice along with guidance and monitoring are more paramount than providing warmth or acceptance. Chao (1994, 2001b) has explained that expectations for or perceptions of warmth involving emotional or physical demonstrativeness (i.e., telling youth, "I love you," hugging them, or even praising them) are particularly rare or are even seen as inappropriate by some Asian immigrant parents. Adolescents from both Chinese and Filipino immigrant families may themselves regard parents' contributions (e.g., paying for education) and sacrifices as a necessary part of parenting, or of showing care and concern. Further research may be needed to test whether Asian American adolescents with parents born in the United States, i.e., second or third generation, and also other ethnic groups of Asian Americans (for example, Korean Americans) endorse these crucial parenting behaviors differently.

The results of this and the two prior chapters provide strong support for the need for more sophisticated culturally based understandings of parenting practices and parent-adolescent relationships. We have identified important cultural group differences in measures related to parental control. At the same time, we show general similarities for the construct of parental support (warmth and acceptance), but as the current chapter has shown, this singular dimension does not incorporate the importance of parental sacrifice as a central dimension of Asian American parental support. In the chapters that follow, we narrow our lens again, focusing on an in-depth, grounded exploration of adolescents' perspectives on each of these dimensions of parenting.

References

Bacho, P. (1997). The tragic sense of Filipino history. In M. P. Root (Ed.), *Filipino Americans: Transformation and identity* (pp. 1–10). Thousand Oaks, CA: Sage Publication.

Blair, S. L., & Qian, Z. (1998). Family and Asian students' educational performance: A consideration of diversity. *Journal of Family Issues, 19*, 355–374.

Bullock, H. E., & Waugh, I. M. (2005). Beliefs about poverty and opportunity among Mexican immigrant farm workers. *Journal of Applied Social Psychology, 35*(6), 1132–1149.

Chao, R. K. (1994). Beyond parental control and authoritarian parenting style: Understanding Chinese parenting through the cultural notion of training. *Child Development, 65*, 1111–1119.

Chao, R. K. (1995). Chinese and European American cultural models of the self reflected in mothers' childrearing beliefs. *Ethos, 23*, 328–354.

Chao, R. K. (2001a). Extending research on the consequences of parenting style for Chinese Americans and European Americans. *Child Development, 72*, 1832–1843.

Chao, R. K. (2001b). Integrating culture and attachment. *American Psychologist, 56*, 822–823.

Chao, R. K., & Tseng, V. (2002). Parenting of Asians. In M. H. Bornstein (Ed.), *Handbook of parenting: Vol. 4: Social conditions and applied parenting* (2nd ed., pp. 59–93). Mahwah, NJ: Lawrence Erlbaum Associates Publishers.

Chen, S. X., Bond, M. H., & Tang, D. (2007). Decomposing filial piety into filial attitude and filial enactments. *Asian Journal of Social Psychology, 10*, 213–223.

Cheung, C., Kwan, A., & Ng, S. H. (2006). Impacts of filial piety on preference for kinship versus public care. *Journal of Community Psychology, 34*(5), 617–634.

Crockett, L. J., Randall, B. A., Shen, Y., Russell, S. T., & Driscoll, A. K. (2005). Measurement equivalence of the center for epidemiological studies depression scale for Latino and Anglo adolescents: A national study. *Journal of Consulting and Clinical Psychology, 73*, 47–58.

Espiritu, Y. L. (1995). *Filipino American lives*. Philadelphia, PA: Temple University Press.

Fuligni, A. J., & Yoshikawa, H. (2002). Investments in children among immigrant families. In A. Kalil & T. DeLeire (Eds.), *Family investments in children's potential: Resources and parenting behavior that promote success*. Mahwah, NJ: Lawrence Erlbaum.

Grotevant, H. D. (1987). Toward a process model of identity formation. *Journal of Adolescent Research, 2*, 203–222.

Hardway, C., & Fuligni, A. J. (2006). Dimensions of family connectiveness among adolescents with Mexican, Chinese, and European backgrounds. *Developmental Psychology, 42*(6), 1246–1258.

Hui, C. H., & Triandis, H. C. (1985). Measurement in cross-cultural psychology. *Journal of Cross-Cultural Psychology, 16*, 131–152.

Hyman, I., Vu, N., & Beiser, M. (2001). Post-migration stress among Southeast Asian refugee youth in Canada: A research note. *Journal of Comparative Family Studies, 31*, 281–293.

Julian, T. W., McHenry, P. C., & McKelvey, M. W. (1994). Cultural variations in parenting, perceptions of Caucasian, African American, Hispanic, and Asian American parents. *Family Relations, 43*, 30–37.

Kim, K., & Rohner, R. P. (2002). Parental warmth, control, and involvement in schooling: Predicting academic achievement among Korean American adolescents. *Journal of Cross-Cultural Psychology, 33*(2), 127–140.

Kitano, H. H. L., & Daniels, R. (1995). *Asian Americans: Emerging minorities* (2nd ed.). Englewood Cliffs, NJ: Prentice Hall.

Lan, P.-C. (2002). Subcontracting filial piety. *Journal of Family Issues, 23*(7), 812–835.

Lansford, J. E., Chang, L., Dodge, K. A., Malone, P. S., Oburu, P., Palmerus, K., et al. (2005). Physical discipline and children's adjustment: Cultural normativeness as a moderator. *Child Development, 76*, 1129–1317.

Muthén, B. O. (1984). A general structural equation model with dichotomous, ordered, categorical, and continuous latent variable indicators. *Psychometrika, 49*, 115–132.

Muthén, L. K., & Muthén, B. O. (2008). *Mplus*. Los Angeles, CA: Muthén and Muthén.

Nunnaly, J. (1978). *Psychometric theory*. New York: McGraw-Hill.

Park, M., & Chelsa, C. (2007). Revisiting Confucianism as a conceptual framework for Asian family study. *Journal of Family Nursing, 13*(3), 293–311.

Parmar, P., & Rohner, R. P. (2008). Relations among spouse acceptance, remembered parental acceptance in childhood and psychological adjustment among married adults in India. *Cross-Cultural Research, 42*(1), 57–66.

Pyke, K. (2000). "The normal American family" as an interpretive structure of family life among grown children of Korean and Vietnamese immigrants. *Journal of Marriage and the Family, 62*, 240–255.

Rohner, R. P. (1960). *Child acceptance-rejection and modal personality in three Pacific societies*. Unpublished masters thesis, Stanford University, Stanford.

Rohner, R. P. (1975). *They love me, they love me not: A worldwide study of the effects of parental acceptance and rejection*. New Haven, CT: HRAF Press.

Rohner, R. P., Khaleque, A., & Cournoyer, D. E. (2005). Parental acceptance-rejection: Theory, methods, cross-cultural evidence, and implications. *Ethos, 33*(3), 299–334.

Schaefer, E. S. (1959). A circumplex model for maternal behavior. *Journal of Abnormal and Social Psychology, 59*, 226–235.

Schaefer, E. S. (1965a). Children's reports of parental behavior: An inventory. *Child Development, 36*(2), 413–424.

Schaefer, E. S. (1965b). A configurational analysis of children's report on parent behavior. *Journal of Consulting Psychology, 29*(6), 552–557.

Schludermann, E. H., & Schludermann, S. M. (1970). Replicability of factors in children's report of parent behavior (CRPBI). *Journal of Psychology: Interdisciplinary and Applied, 76*(2), 239–249.

Schludermann, E. H., & Schludermann, S. M. (1983). Sociocultural change and adolescents' perceptions of parent behavior. *Developmental Psychology, 19*(5), 674–685.

Schludermann, E. H., & Schludermann, S. M. (1988). *Children's report on parent behavior* (CRPBI-108, CRPBI-30 for children and older adolescents, Technical Report). Winnipeg, MB, Canada: University of Manitoba.

Wu, C. (2007). *Intergenerational cultural distance in parenting-adolescent relationship among Chinese immigrants*. Unpublished PhD dissertation, University of California, Riverside, CA.

Chapter 5
The Meanings of Parent-Adolescent Relationship Quality Among Chinese American and Filipino American Adolescents

Stephen T. Russell, June Y. Chu, Lisa J. Crockett, and Stacey N. Doan

The prior chapters (and a growing body of research) suggest important ethnic differences in parenting practices and parent-adolescent relationship quality. This work documents systematic ethnic and cultural group differences in survey measurement of key constructs of parenting, yet little is known about the cultural meanings of parenting that are held by young people. Studies based on European American families in the United States have shown that "good parenting" includes the characteristics of warmth, affection, responsiveness, involvement, and firmness, and that such parenting practices promote independence and autonomy in children (Lawton, Schuler, Fowell, & Madsen, 1984; Steinberg, 2001). However, studies of Asian and Asian American families suggest that "good parents" are those who provide and sacrifice for, nurture, and monitor adolescents' activities (Xiong, Eliason, Detzner, & Cleveland, 2005), whereas good behavior on the part of children includes collectivistic qualities of family obligation, filial piety and reciprocity (Cooper, Baker, Polichar, & Welsh, 1993; Ho, 1986), and acceptance of or obedience to parental authority (Chen & Yang, 1986; Hsu, 1981). These cultural differences are thought to be the basis for ethnic group differences in the meaning and implications of parenting practices for adolescents.

Little prior research directly investigates the meanings associated with parent-adolescent relationships or parenting practices from the perspectives of Asian Americans. However, the results of prior survey-based research suggest the possibility of a deeper understanding of the ways that Asian American adolescents understand and experience relationships with parents. For example, the prior chapter shows that parental sacrifice is a central component of parental support for Chinese American and Filipino American adolescents. The results of Chapter 3 show that Chinese American adolescents report lower parental warmth than European American adolescents. The second chapter indicates that, in the national sample studied, measures of parental support hold similar meaning for European and

S.T. Russell (✉)
University of Arizona, Tucson, AZ, USA
e-mail: strussell@arizona.edu

S.T. Russell et al. (eds.), *Asian American Parenting and Parent-Adolescent Relationships*, Advancing Responsible Adolescent Development,
DOI 10.1007/978-1-4419-5728-3_5,

Filipino American adolescents (although for boys there may be subtle differences in the salience of paternal behaviors within an overall construct of paternal support). However, the same measures were not applicable to Chinese American adolescent boys or girls, who may have markedly different conceptual structures for understanding parental support. Chao and Padmawidjaja (in Chapter 3; see also Wu & Chao, 2005) suggest that Asian American adolescents' reports of parenting may be guided by their understanding of their families' Asian cultures as well as by dominant U.S. cultural images of parent-adolescent relationships. Thus, a qualitative investigation of the ways Asian American adolescents describe and understand their relationships with parents may provide a more complete understanding of the results of prior studies.

Parenting practices are said to reflect the quality of relationships between parents and children (Chao, 2001). In this chapter we present results from a study designed to elicit understandings of parental support from Asian American adolescents. In order to capture adolescents' perspectives on supportive parenting, we conducted focus group interviews with Chinese American and Filipino American adolescents, asking them what it meant to have a good relationship with parents.

Method

Sample

Participating students were recruited through youth group organizations in a major metropolitan area in northern California. Students were paid $30 for their participation in the focus group session. Eight focus groups were conducted; two focus groups with each sex of each ethnic group (boys and girls of Chinese American and Filipino American) included a total of 40 participants. The focus groups were held after school hours in two locations (focus groups for Chinese and Filipino boys and girls were conducted at both locations): at a high school in a central suburb, and at a high school in an out lying suburban town. The central suburban school is located in an ethnically mixed neighborhood of the city, with a larger proportion of Asian American students from many ethnic backgrounds. It can be characterized as middle class. The students that attend the high school in the outlying town come from families that are mostly working class and poor. Although the students were recruited through youth organizations, participants lived in the communities local to the schools where the focus groups were conducted.

Recruitment criteria for participation in the group included: attending high school, English speaking, living with at least one parent, having at least one parent who was born outside of the USA (all participants were second generation, with the exception of one third-generation Filipina), and being a member of a specified ethnic minority group (Filipino American or Chinese American). Twenty-one of the students were in the 12th grade; the rest were in 11th grade. The mean age was 16.9 years. All of the female participants lived with both parents in the same household; two of the Chinese American boys and four of the Filipino American boys lived with their mothers only. Five of the Chinese American boys, two of the Filipino American boys, and one Filipina American girl had no siblings. Eleven of the students spoke only English at home with their families, while the majority (25) spoke a combination of English and another language at home; three of the Chinese boys spoke non-English at home (one reported speaking Mandarin and 2 reported Cantonese), and one Filipina girl spoke only Tagalog at home. All of the participating students completed a self-report demographic questionnaire which was administered at the beginning of the focus group session; all were fluent in English and able to participate fully in the focus group discussion.

Interviews and Measures

Procedure. Consent was obtained from parents and adolescents prior to participation in the study. Each room was equipped with a large conference table, paper and pencil (at each seat) for note-taking, audiotape equipment, and large butcher paper (for the moderator and assistant to make notes on for participants to see). All sessions were audio-taped for later transcription. Two assistants were present at all sessions to take comprehensive notes about participants' expressions and unclear responses, and to set up the room for each session.

A trained Asian American female served as the moderator for the groups. In addition to posing questions to the group, the moderator was responsible for ensuring ease of conversation and establishing rapport among group members. The moderator for the focus groups had ample experience serving as a moderator, and also possessed an adequate background of the subject matter under discussion. Open-ended questions were worded with specific ethnic groups in mind: "For Filipino American teens, what does it mean for a teen to have a good relationship with her/his mother?" During the discussion two specific probes were used, including "How do you know if a teenager has a good relationship with their mom?" and "How would a teen describe a good relationship with their mother?" Next, participants were asked to review and comment on the survey items measuring parental support and autonomy-granting from the Add Health study (see Chapter 2). Following discussion of mother-adolescent relationships, the same questions were asked regarding relationships with fathers.

The moderator would first ask the question and encourage spontaneous responses. Participants were reminded that honest and truthful answers would be most helpful to the discussion. If a response was unclear, the moderator would ask for further clarification. Although participants were not discouraged from talking about their own personal experiences, they were encouraged to speak from the perspective of all youth in their ethnic group. In post-focus group process notes and de-briefing discussions, the moderator did not indicate that audio-taping and note-taking adversely affected the responses. Each focus group lasted approximately an hour and a half to 2 hours.

Analytic Method

The focus group interviews were audio-taped and transcribed to facilitate a process of selecting and reducing the data of interest into manageable units in order to detect thematic patterns (Miles & Huberman, 1994). Working in pairs, research team members read sections of the transcripts that corresponded to the guiding questions of the focus group interview (good relationships with mother; good relationships with father). Consistent with methods outlined by LeCompte and Schensul (1999), coding teams derived coding themes from the transcript data and organized quotes into categories representing those themes. The full research team discussed themes, considered alternative interpretations, and resolved, by consensus, differences in individual opinions regarding interpretations or representations. Presentation of results focuses on thematic categories representing ideas that were frequently mentioned as well as those that were unique and provide insight into the diversity (rather than generalizability) of Asian American adolescents' understandings of good parent-adolescent relationships.

Results

Adolescents' discussions of good relationships with mothers and fathers were clearly gendered, that is, Chinese and Filipina American girls' discussions of good parental relationships were more similar to one another than they were to boys from their same ethnic groups. Further, maternal relationships were described much differently than were paternal relationships. For girls, good mother-daughter relationships were characterized by communication and trust, "just knowing" that mothers care, and for Filipina American girls, the possibility of mother-daughter friendship. Good relationships with fathers were more difficult for adolescent girls to describe; although girls indicated that communication and closeness were important, they often felt that these qualities were absent in relationships with fathers.

Different patterns emerged in discussions with boys. Good relationships with mothers were described by maternal sacrifices, by communication, and, specifically for Filipino American boys, by trust. Good paternal relationships were characterized by communication, guidance, and respect for fathers among Chinese American boys; Filipino American boys also described communication, but talked about guidance in terms of fathers' strength and discussed the importance of friendship with fathers, a dimension that was not discussed by Chinese American boys.

Mother-Daughter Relationships

Communication and trust. When defining a good relationship with mothers, the first responses given by both Chinese American and Filipina American girls identified good communication and trust as central to good maternal relationships. As one Chinese American girl stated, "good communication is number one . . . ," or as one Filipina American girl said, "I think mostly just like talking with your mom . . . be able to like trust her with certain things or feel that she'd be a confidante." Although each of the focus groups began with these themes of communication and trust, there were distinct differences between the ways that Chinese American and Filipina American girls elaborated on these ideas.

For Chinese American girls, respect and honor for elders, including filial obligation, was a foundation that provided the possibility for communication and trust in mother-daughter relationships. In defining a good relationship one girl said, "I suppose have good communication . . . and also, just the respect that they are your elders and you're not to talk back and do the chores and do well in school, support your parents when they . . . retire and you're working, that you'll be able to support them." Another girl said, "for the mom . . . just being there to talk to and stuff. And for the kid . . . like you're doing chores and just really honoring them, like respecting if they ask, like if my parent would ask me to like not go out maybe for 1 day just 'cause we would like you to stay home, then like respect that too." For these girls, good communication and trust were built from respect that is based on understanding the associated responsibilities across generations. Furthermore, explicit in the quotes is the idea that respect and obedience are integral to the concept of communication. For some of the girls, respect included recognition on their part of the very different adolescent experiences their mothers had compared to their own. One girl said, " . . . both of them (mother and daughter) should be open and trusting and like respect each other. . . . like what teenagers do now, she really doesn't want me to do mostly those things. So, like just more like communication I guess, to understand why I want to do the kinds of things I want to do." In their initial descriptions of a good relationship with mothers, Chinese American girls articulated their understanding of communication and trust as a mutual generational responsibility based on respect.

The discussions with Filipina American girls about maternal communication and trust were quite different in tone. These themes were described as ideals that were not typical among Filipino American mothers and daughters. A recurring theme in both focus groups had to do with mother's strictness: communication and trust were the first ideas mentioned when describing a good relationship with mothers, but they were almost always described in relation to mothers' strictness, or as ways to prevent conflict in the mother-daughter relationship. As one girl explained, "I think communication also and the ability to like understand one another from each point of view . . . if they don't take it through both perspectives then it might cause a problem between the relationship." Another girl said, "I think a daughter should be open with their mother so that the mom can respond to them instead of hiding behind their back and trying to figure out what the daughter's social life is. So I think a good relationship is good communication between the daughter and the mom." Regarding trust another said, "Well, trust also, of course, 'cause they won't let you do anything if there's no trust." For these Filipina American girls, strictness and control on the part of mothers seemed to imply a lack of trust in daughters. Open communication offered the possibility for trust, and the potential for mothers to react by easing their strictness with daughters.

Like the Chinese American girls, the Filipina American girls also spoke of respect. However, the meaning of respect was different for each group. For Filipinas, respect referred to parent control rather than family obligation. One girl described a good relationship as characterized by "trust and respect, of course, 'cause if you have both of those then . . . she'd be lenient on me, she wouldn't be as strict. Like if she didn't trust me, then of course she wouldn't let me—she'd put me on lockdown." Another girl said

> I think it's mostly about respect because . . . the mom is kind of controlling . . . . The mom should be kind of more lenient and just let her go out but then at least like come home at 10:00 or something. But then the daughter has to give her respect by saying okay, 'I'll come home at 10:00 rather than like be late at 10:30 or whatever.' So it's kind of like respecting each other both ways.

From this girl's perspective, respect is understood as mutual in that it provides the basis for mothers to trust their daughters, and to allow them freedom or autonomy in activities and behavior. There is a subtle difference in the ways the girls talk about their mothers, in that the Chinese American girls seem to be more aware of their roles and hierarchy in the relationship, while the Filipina American girls seem to be negotiating independence in their relationships with their mothers.

Maternal strictness was so central to these discussions that Filipina American girls seemed to define good relationships by a mother's regulation of her daughter's freedom and activities. The girls stated that when mothers make rules and goals for their children they are showing that they care; however, often it is "too much." A girl's description of a good mother-daughter relationship began: "Well, it's like kind of obvious like when she makes rules and like goals for you. But like sometimes you just don't want to listen 'cause you just kind of like hate her, I guess, and if she makes you mad and like the more she holds you back, the more you want to like rebel against her." Another girl said, "Sometimes when like they're caring about you, it can be taken the wrong way. Like when my mom asks me like how I'm doing or who I went out with, it's always in an angry confrontational kind of voice." Another said, "I know that she loves me and she's trying to like do it because she loves me, protect me, but kind of like to the point where she doesn't really let me do a lot of stuff that I'm supposed to like experience at this age." Adolescent girls' descriptions of maternal control and mother-daughter conflict are not remarkable; what is interesting here is that Filipina American girls offer these comments in connection with describing a "good" mother-daughter relationship. Strictness and control are integral to the relationship, and therefore the negotiation of maternal control is central to discussions of good relationships.

"You just know" that she cares. In describing how you know if a teenager has a good relationship with her mother, both Chinese American and Filipina American girls said that "you just know" from the things that mothers do for daughters and the

family; for example, instrumental support such as cooking is consistently identified as a way that mothers show that they care. When further probed in discussion, Chinese American girls described mothers as expressing their caring indirectly, through these instrumental activities. Filipina American girls, on the other hand, again discussed maternal strictness, and a concern with school and boyfriends as signs of caring.

All of the girls cited instances where mothers show their concern or care for children by providing daily, instrumental support. Mothers do things for their daughters—driving them places, shopping, and cooking. For both Chinese American and Filipina American girls, cooking played a large role in mothers' caring. One Filipina American girl said, "I know my mom cares about me when she cooks 'cause she doesn't cook. But she's like, 'Oh do you want some vegetables?' Then it's like wow, my mom cooked! I'm like hey guys, my mom cooked." Another Filipina American girl said, "Like if she cooks . . . the stuff that's in the box, it's like she's just trying to feed you, but when she cooks from scratch or on her days off if she's cooking the whole day and then . . . she sets the table and stuff, it's like . . . I really know that she cares." Several of the Chinese American girls also mentioned cooking and other supportive tasks that their mothers would perform: "Well, she takes me to school . . . she picks me up when I need to. She takes me places that I need to go to and, you know, shopping with me is a hassle but . . . she is willing to do it. And like she cooks for me every night. If I need help with something, she's there to help." Another Chinese American girl talks about the things her mother does in terms of sacrifice for the family, saying "She really likes to drive us around. She's like: 'you're going to college soon, you know. I really like to take you places.' . . . she still wants to drive me 'cause she just really, you know, likes being with us . . . or like the stuff she'll sacrifice, you know, to do for me. I can really see that." For this girl the mother's sacrifices for the family are the basis for knowing that she cares, and are what defines a good relationship.

Instrumental support from mothers appears to take the place of the verbal communication of caring; the idea of verbally expressing love or support was only raised to explain that it did not happen. Two Chinese American girls said that their mothers do not communicate love directly. One said, "it's kind of weird because my entire life she's never said three words, 'I love you,' but . . . the way she talks to me and the things she does for me, you know . . . like it shows." Later in the discussion another Chinese American girl said, "I want to elaborate on what [she] said how—it's like my mom never says 'I love you' either. But I mean, it's just the simple things that she does . . . I mean, I'm happy with the relationship I have with her because . . . we don't exactly say sorry when we fight or when we end a fight. We just go back to the way that things were . . . nobody says anything." Both girls seem to want to explain why their mothers never say, "I love you." However, one Chinese American girl said, "well, my family, we're a huggy family . . . yeah, my mom gives us hugs and stuff like that." This was the only time that verbal or physical affection was mentioned by a Chinese American girl. Thus, for most Chinese American girls, verbal expressions of love are an important indicator of good mother-daughter relationships; however, they are not a necessity, because love and care are expressed in nonverbal ways, through actions.

The issue of maternal strictness came up again for Filipina American girls when they discussed the ways you know that a mother cares. A caring mother is one who imposes rules: "when they set limits you know they care about you because they care about your well-being." When asked how you know if your mom loves you and cares about you one Filipina American girl said, "well, it's like kind of obvious like when she makes rules and like goals for you." One specific topic that came up a number of times among Filipina American girls was that of boyfriends. The girls described keeping secrets about boyfriends, saying that their mothers "couldn't handle it" and that acknowledging boyfriends would damage their relationship with their mother. Although mothers' rules and worries are frustrating, one girl noted that "if your mom didn't care, if she just lets you go off, do drugs and leave the house at 2:00 o'clock in the morning, that means she doesn't care about you. That means she's not worried about you." In general, although Filipina American girls seemed to complain about their mothers' worries and control over their behavior, this control was interpreted as caring and understood as characteristic of a good relationship.

Mother-daughter friendship. In one of the focus groups with Filipina American girls a comparison was made to mother-daughter relationships in European American and Black families. One girl said, "I think White people are more open to each other. They more have like: 'Oh, yeah, Mom, I have a boyfriend.' 'Oh, really, wow, great.' But no, not for Filipino Americans. It's different, it's like: 'Who? What's their name, what's their address, what's their phone number?'" This led to a discussion of a popular television show, *The Gilmore Girls*. The girls in the focus group described the show as focusing on a White mother and daughter who are best characterized as friends. One Filipina American girl commented on how she wishes her relationship with her mother were like the mother-daughter relationship on the show, and discusses differences between White and Filipino American families: "Like Rory and Lorelei, they're like friends first . . . they're both really good people and I admire their relationship and I wish mine was like that, too. Because they're just like so close." In the following exchange between two Filipina American girls, one talks positively about mother-daughter friendship, whereas the second challenges the idea:

Speaker 1: My African American friends and their parents, they're friends first before mother and daughter and daughter and mother. They're friends first. And I think that's cool because then that makes, gives you the opportunity to . . . have a better relationship.

Speaker 2: I don't think the friends first is kind of good because what if the daughter starts trying to take advantage of the mother? So it's kinda like the mother has to be kind of a little bit of both.

Thus, the girls suggest that a mother-daughter relationship characterized by friendship is an ideal. However, they indicate that not only do they not have this type of relationship with their mothers, they do not imagine Filipino American mothers and daughters relating in this way.

The idea that your mother might be your friend was also mentioned by several of the Chinese American girls; in one focus group session, Chinese American girls also discussed *The Gilmore Girls* when talking about good mother-daughter relationships. One girl said:

> Like one of my friends, her and her mom, they will go out to watch a movie, just them two, and so I guess it's like besides mother/daughter relationship there's like a friendship involved in it. Like not in the extreme—I don't know if you've ever heard of the television show *Gilmore Girls*—not to that extreme, but it's just that there's a friendship between the mom and daughter instead of like my mom takes care of me and that.

This girl suggests that friendship is both an ideal, but that the ideal is "extreme." When other Chinese American girls mentioned friendship they talked about it as an ideal that is not realistic in mother-daughter relationships. For both Filipina and Chinese American girls, friendship was not realistic, and for some not appropriate, for mother-daughter relationships.

Father-Daughter Relationships

One Chinese American girl's initial response to the questions about a good father-daughter relationship was, "This one is so much harder." In each of the focus groups the girls talked about fathers as economic providers for their families: "He'll always make sure that I'm like well taken care of." Aside from this role as provider, both the Chinese American and Filipina American girls emphasized emotional closeness or communication in their descriptions of good father-daughter relationships. For example, one Chinese American girl said, "he's willing to listen to you," but this was said in a speculative manner (as opposed to describing the reality of her situation). She continues:

> ...every time I try to talk to my dad he just sticks to one thing and he keeps talking about that, like it's really, really bad. And then so I can't tell him the rest of my story or whatever I wanted to tell him. And then he just finds little things to get mad at me.... So I mean, I don't really know how a good father would be because I've never really had one. And I've never heard anyone else who's had one 'cause every time I talk to my friends, like yeah, I went with my mom to dah, dah, dah. They never say oh, I went with my dad.

This girl understands that her relationship with her father is not a "good" one, as she is unable to communicate effectively with him, but also admits that she has yet to see a good father-daughter relationship.

One Chinese American girl said, "maybe I'm just assuming, but from what I hear from like friends and everything, Chinese American daughters usually tend to be more close with their mothers than their fathers for some reason." The focus group moderator asked what others thought, and they all agreed. Except for a few girls who described their fathers as explicitly punitive and unkind and one girl who talked about her father as unique in being affectionate, the Chinese American girls generally agreed that their fathers are "nice," but emotionally closed off. Other research on Asian American adolescents indicates that communication with fathers may be particularly difficult (Rhee, Chang, & Rhee, 2003). "Like yeah, he blocks himself from his family.... I feel like sometimes he like pushes me away." Another Chinese American girl described distance in the relationship with her father as follows:

> Personally, I don't think I'm really close to my dad. Like—well, for me, like it's uncomfortable to be in the same room as him sometimes, especially after like something happens. ... So like me and my dad, we're just kind of really distant and we don't talk like in depth about anything or ... I know he cares 'cause like obviously like your mom and dad, like when they show that they're worried, you know, or they're willing to help you do something you know that they care. But... with my mom I'm a lot closer. With my dad... we're just kind of distant.

Another Chinese American girl described the ways that she feels compelled to limit communication with her father:

> My father, he's nice to me, he's really nice but the communication, it just has to be closed for us because if he knew everything then I think—he's really innocent, the way he thinks, and he thinks that I just go to school, I'm really good. I have no guy friends, you know, I'm just a really good person. And he just wants it to be that way. And sometimes I think about it. I'd rather have him think that way than who I really am.... I really think he can't handle the truth about the teenage Americans. He can't handle it.

In this case it is the daughter who creates distance. She argues that she needs to keep secrets from her immigrant father to protect him; she describes an irreconcilable clash between the worlds of immigrant fathers and American daughters.

Filipina American girls also talked about communication and emotional closeness with fathers, but in more affirmative terms than the Chinese American girls. A Filipina American girl stated, "Well, for me it's kinda hard for me to be open with my dad 'cause he's more strict, but he shows how he cares like when he gives me hugs and when he kisses me before I go to sleep or before I leave the house for school or work." For this girl her father's strictness prompted her to limit openness, but at the same time she described an affectionate relationship with her father. Another Filipina American girl stressed the importance of conversations, saying that they are a way for fathers to express affection: "When you talk to—or when your dad tries to talk to you or you guys have conversations, that's when you know he cares and that's like one of the ways he shows affection, by like trying to talk to you as in getting to know you and with trying to teach you something. Even though it may be boring, they're really trying to like tell you something for real." Another Filipina American girl contrasted communication with her father versus mother saying, "I'm closer to my dad than my mom.... I can like actually like talk to him because he won't yell at me. He'll just talk to me. He won't punish me. The way he like punishes me is just by like talking to me. He doesn't like hit me or like ground me. He'll just like talk it out on me." Even though this girl framed the discussion of communication with her father in terms of less risk of punishment, she clearly stated that her relationship with her father is closer than her relationship with her mother.

Other Filipina American girls talked more directly about their affective relationships with their fathers. In the following, the first girl talks about her own father's emotional distance, while the second describes this as being culturally typical:

*Speaker*1: Like if my grand-grandpa died or like we lost our house or something, then he would be warm and loving. But he doesn't like show how he's affected emotionally.

*Speaker*2: ... like she said, that it's not really like acceptable in our society. But there are times when my dad's like—when my dad'll just give me a hug, but I think most of the time without thinking about it I take it the wrong way. Like I'm like, "What do you want?" you know, and then I think about it later and I'm like I shouldn't have done that, but it's just 'cause it's not something that I'm used to or that most people are used to, like your dad giving you a hug.

Here the second speaker suggests that with Filipino American families, fathers are not expected to be affectionate and in fact her understanding of this expectation caused her to question her father's displays of affection.

The idea that the father-daughter relationship could be characterized as a friendship was only discussed by Filipina American girls. "I think I'm closer to him... because he's more of a friend and he can talk to me as if I'm, he's one of my guy friends and he can tell me things that my mom wouldn't have told me and I guess that's why." Another girl said she knows when Filipino American teens have good relationships with their fathers, "I think it's when they act like friends or they kick it, you know, they hang out. That's when I know that they have a good relationship." Another girl said, "I can tell when people have good relationships with their dads when they're just—I think it's usually humor that indicates that. Like when I see my friends, if they joke around with their dad, it shows that they can be open and they can just be blunt about stuff with their dads. I think it's that humor." At several other points Filipina American girls talked about humor, joking around, or acting like friends with fathers as defining a good relationship. On the other hand, Chinese American girls never expressed these sentiments.

Several common themes emerged for Chinese American and Filipino American girls. Apparent in their responses is an understanding of what might constitute an "ideal relationship" as influenced by Western culture (e.g., open communication, trust, friendship, affect), but also the girl's sense that their relationships are qualitatively different from what might be described as the American ideal. Both groups of girls described communication and trust as central to relationships with mothers. However, Filipina Americans were more inclined to also bring up maternal strictness as related to topics of communication and trust. Maternal care is an important facet of the mother-daughter relationship, although care is not demonstrative (e.g., overt showing of affection), but rather instrumental in nature. When mothers care for you and show that they care by providing for you, they are demonstrating love without needing to explicitly state it. Finally, although the idea of friendship between mothers and daughters is one that is appealing in some ways, both groups of girls seem to understand that this is not a reality for them, and to some degree that this may be inappropriate in its extreme. Relationships with fathers were more complicated for both groups of girls to describe. First and foremost, fathers were considered providers who offered the financial means in which to support the family. Beyond this we found a difference in how girls could describe father-daughter relationships—although some fathers were described as distant (by both Chinese American and Filipina American girls), some of the Filipina Americans characterized the relationship as more friend-like in quality.

Mother-Son Relationships

Need to protect. When defining a good relationship with their mothers, Chinese American boys and Filipino American boys both discussed the things that mothers actively do for them. Unlike the girls, who described a reciprocal or mutual responsibility for good mother-daughter relationships, the boys suggested that mothers are responsible for creating a good relationship, and that they establish a good mother-son relationship by showing they care through their worrying and need to overprotect. One Filipino boy described Filipino mothers, "Filipino moms, like they really care about their sons and like they're like sometimes they're overprotective... that's what I observe about my cousins' moms," and one Chinese boy similarly described mothers' need to worry, "I think the thing is that the moms really care and worry about their child.... and with the news these days they hear like a lot of bad things going on outside in the world so they worry about their child." Thus, these boys take their mothers' worries as evidence of caring.

Demonstration of care. A good relationship as described by these boys involved mothers *showing* that they care. Mothers were described by the Chinese American boys as making sacrifices and providing psychological, physical, and financial support. According to one boy, "she goes to work and then comes home, cooks for the whole family and then she probably doesn't—she goes to sleep late but then she also does a lot of housework." Another Chinese boy described how mothers show their care by fulfilling maternal duties: "I feel like she fulfills her duties as being a mother and she gives me the space that I need. And she does her duties... she goes to work, she cooks, she just—she takes me shopping, she buys whatever and she—she cares, she wants to know where I am. She—yeah, she cares." Filipino American boys indicate that mothers show they care through instrumental support. "Like I know my mom cares about me like when I come home from school like right away when I open the door it's, 'Are you hungry?' Like she'll go to my room and I'll wonder what she's doing in there and like she'll be trying to tidy up my room instead of me having to do it 'cause like she wants me to stay focused on my schoolwork. So I see that she cares a lot." Another boy also described mothers as providers of moral guidance, "Me and my mom like we got a real good bond 'cause like back in my younger years like I used to go in the wrong direction. Like if it wasn't for her she would—I wouldn't have been able to get back on track, to maintain, to stay and love myself." Thus, similar to the girls, the boys supported the notion that mothers show they care through behaviors and not through words.

Friendship and trust. To describe a good relationship with mothers, Chinese American boys discussed the importance of friendship and feeling comfortable with mothers. They noted that if you are not embarrassed by your mother in public, you have a good relationship with her. As one Chinese boy put it, "I think a good relationship with your mom is being able to go out places with her and not be embarrassed, and you can talk to her like a friend." This type of friendship was distinct from the ideal mother-daughter relationship described by Asian American girls who talked about mutuality as unrealistic.

For the Filipino American boys, trust was mentioned as important to a good mother-son relationship rather than friendship. Trusting your mother is important because it is mutual—to trust, you have to be trusted, and this is the foundation on which the relationship can be built. As one boy described it, "I trust my mom a lot, like I tell her well, like whenever I have problems and sort of she's like whenever I have a problem, [the] first person I go to so I don't think about it anyone," and another boy, "When you trust—you have trust in your mom and your mom trusts you. I think that's key." One Filipino boy discussed trust as the foundation on which communication between mothers and sons can be established, "If it clearly shows that there's trust in the relationship, I'd say that it could show good relations with the mother and also they're open to talk about like some things that have happened."

Guidance and control. While Chinese American boys discussed mothers as friends, Filipino American boys intimated the high levels of control that Filipino mothers exert. Filipino mothers were described as having high expectations for their children, and also as being teachers, particularly in the moral domain. One boy described Filipino mothers as follows: "I think like all Filipino moms, like they expect a lot out of you and like they want you to succeed like in school so—yeah, I have that with my parents too and with my mom." Another boy explained that mothers exert control even when they are not present, "say, you're tempted to do something bad, like the first thing that'll pop in your mind would just be seeing mom's face in your head like 'She always tells me not to do this.'"

In contrast, Chinese mothers exerted control over their sons by asking questions, something that also indicated they care. Responding to the question of how you know mothers care, the Chinese American boys explained, "Well, usually the mother is protective of their child so they'll ask many questions." For Chinese American boys, maternal concern was related to the number of questions that mothers asked, and was intertwined with protectiveness. The nuance here is that maternal questioning is somewhat deferential; whereas Filipina American mothers let their sons know that they worry and tell them what to do, Chinese mothers show these same feelings through asking their sons.

Communication. Lastly, the Chinese and Filipino American boys discussed communication between mothers and sons. Communication was very important to the Chinese American boys in establishing a good relationship with their mothers. Boys stated the importance of a "good habit of communicating, like a good habit of understanding each other," and that "communication is a big part of the whole relationship." One boy discussed the unidirectional character of communication with his mother, stating: "Like you can have a good relationship in a way that—like for me, my mom, I know she really cares and she always asks me questions. But . . . I kind of see it as like really bothering and I don't want to take the time to answer all these questions." Here communication is the way to create a good relationship, but at the same time it can be irritating. This boy went on to say that his mother initiates communication but he pushes her away, "sometimes at the moment I just react to it that way where I kind of push her away. And so like—it's not that they don't want to be close to you."

Filipino American boys discussed communication in relation to trust and mutual respect.

> For me, I think a good relation with like your mom would be like . . . you guys have trust in each other and everything you know. You know, like just basically no fighting or anything and you guys understand good like communication between one another. I mean before I didn't really have a good relationship with my mom but, you know, as I got older I got smarter and everything so I learned to respect my mom and everything and I understand where she's coming from now and she kind of understands where I'm coming from now.

This boy talked about the importance of respect and maturity as contributors to communication and mother-son relationships.

Some of the Filipino American boys reported good communication with their mothers. As one boy stated, "We talk. Like we talk every day when I see her." Others described the limitations of their communication, either due to subject matter of their mother's work schedules: "But yeah, we talk sometimes when—but she's always at work so we never talk now. My relationship with my mom is we talk, but then it's not as personal as other relationships with other mothers are." Other Filipino American boys, however, discussed difficulties in communication with their mothers. One boy cited language differences: "She doesn't have all the words to express what she's feeling . . . so it's hard for us to communicate some ideas sometimes." As with the other groups, the Filipino American boys stated that mothers do not come out and verbalize their love, rather, they show their love and concern by doing things for them.

Father-Son Relationships

Communication. When discussing relationships with fathers, Filipino and Chinese American boys both brought up communication as a part of their relationships. Chinese American boys emphasized their ease of communication, with the father as integral to a good father-son relationship. As one boy stated, "You're able to talk about anything;" another boy confirmed this, stating, "you can tell him everything." Chinese American boys also discussed the gendered nature of communication with fathers, and that although a good relationship with either parent involves open communication, boys are able to talk about more with their fathers (than their mothers) since fathers can understand a boy's perspective. One Chinese boy stated, "You can tell him everything. Maybe this is a point of view as a boy." For the Chinese American boys, communication with fathers was comfortable, and Chinese

American boys considered fathers to be open-minded and able to take different perspectives. This comfort appeared to be largely due to the similarity in gender. One boy stated, "I feel that it's hard to be close with my dad because he's that kind of like enforcer, but like it's easier to talk to him because he's a guy." Thus, fathers might be more difficult to get close to, but communication was not a problem because fathers and sons are of the same gender.

Similar to the Chinese American boys, the Filipino American boys also discussed communication in father-son relationships. Here, however, the boys began by explaining that communication is difficult because in Filipino culture, fathers do not talk a great deal. As this boy puts it,

> I mean for like Filipinos I think it's different 'cause like I have a problem with my father 'cause he doesn't really talk a lot and so my sister tells me that like a lot of our uncles are like that too, and I just notice that they don't talk a lot like with their families or like with their children.

Whereas the Chinese American boys did not see cultural norms as a hindrance to father-son communication, the Filipino American boys indicated that family communication is influenced by Filipino culture.

The Filipino American boys also discussed the gendered nature of communication between fathers and sons. Because of their shared gender, boys presume fathers to have had similar experiences, and are therefore able to discuss certain issues. In particular, the Filipino American boys feel that in a good father-son relationship, sons are able to openly communicate about relationships with girls. One Filipino boy stated: "a good relationship with I guess my dad . . . is somebody you could go to to talk about similar things that you both went through like relationships or how to get a girl or things like that." Another Filipino boy supported the idea that communication is gendered by stating that "the relationship with the father is kind of similar to the relationship with the mother except the difference is [you can] talk to him about how to get a girl and like relationship-wise." Thus, although father-son communication might be constrained as a function of the culture, shared gender roles and experiences could circumvent this gap in communication.

Respect. A second theme that was important for Chinese American boys was respect. When asked what it means for a teen to have a good relationship with their father, one boy immediately responded with, "When they respect their decisions. And then just listens to what he says and takes it as like good advice." In good father-son relationships, boys are expected to take fathers' advice, and to show them respect. One boy stated directly that he has more respect for his father than his mother because of what his father had done for him. Another Chinese boy suggested that respect arises because fathers are in charge: "sometimes you respect your father more 'cause he's like you might see him as more of the head of the household." Chinese fathers are afforded respect from their sons based on their family status as the head of household. For Chinese American boys, hierarchy within the family appears to remain a prevalent theme that is intertwined with respect.

Teacher and Role Model. Whereas the Chinese American boys talked about respect in relation to the family hierarchy, the Filipino American boys discussed the idea of fathers as role models and friends—a theme not found among the Chinese American boys. One boy stated, "my father was like a really good friend to me. He taught me a lot of stuff." This Filipino boy's statement about his father's friendship was followed by discussion of his father's role as a teacher: "a father should prepare you for the real world, kind of like school. He should teach you some of the skills that you need. … I think the father should also help you develop your mind." Another Filipino boy stated, "To me a good relationship with the father is the teacher and the supporter." Filipino American boys saw fathers not only as teachers, but as role models for them to emulate. One boy talked about how sons share their fathers' beliefs, stating, "either you believe what he believes and like you stick up for him and you—cause you want to be like him." In sharing beliefs, then, sons also show their desire to be like their fathers, and as another Filipino boy put it, a good relationship is when you "follow in his footsteps."

In contrast, when the Chinese American boys talked about fathers as teachers, they described the teaching role in terms of respect. One Chinese boy described how his father used to teach him things (such as fishing and culture) and stated that this led him to respect his father. It appears that the Chinese American boys give fathers respect because they see fathers as more knowledgeable than themselves. One boy stated:

> They want to teach their son everything that they know and probably still have their son excel at it so then they can pass that skill on, and like my dad, he knows how to fix things and cook and do all sorts of things so he's trying to teach my brother and I these things.

Another boy confirmed the idea that Chinese fathers are teachers by stating,

> Starting young they just teach you everything you know so when you grow up that's what you know, it always leads to that thing… he would always teach me how to take care of myself and he just tells me, "Oh, don't do this, don't do that," and he just taught me a lot of ethics, like moral ethics.

The Chinese and Filipino American boys saw their fathers' responsibilities as preparing them for the future by sharing their wisdom and knowledge so that their sons could succeed in life. Chinese American boys saw their fathers as teachers, not only in the practical domain, but also in the moral domain. Filipino American boys, on the other hand, saw teaching as a part of their relationship with fathers who serve as role models.

Affect. The Chinese American boys discussed the role of affect in ways that are consistent with their understanding of the hierarchical structure of the Chinese family. One Chinese boy stated that no matter what type of negative affect a father may be showing, a father always cares: "I know my dad cares for me… no matter how much you mess up, like they're just, help you out of it. And then even though they're mad, it doesn't seem like they're mad at you." In this statement, the care that boys believed fathers have for their children is evident; superficial affect such as anger does not preclude care for children. It is also apparent in their discussions that gender is relevant for understanding father's affect. A Chinese American boy commented:

> I think it's kind of the same way you should have with your mom or your mother but yeah, with your father it should also be the same way but in a more rougher way because it just seems kind of awkward, you know, how you're trying to get girly, or the way you kind of get lovey-dovey with your mom.

Not only does this speaker contrast his relationship with his father with the one that he has with his mother, but he also states that sons must act more "manly" or less physical with fathers because this is more comfortable.

Although the Filipino American boys did not bring up affect as a topic that is related to good father-son relationships, they were like the Chinese American boys in their view that father-son relationships have a gendered, masculine quality. Fathers were responsible for instilling masculinity in their sons. One participant stated, "if you don't have a father figure ... you'll miss out on some stuff like you won't have some qualities that some other guy kids have." Another Filipino participant implied that a good relationship with one's father is devoid of femininity, and likewise another boy stated, "The dad figure always has to be stronger, not show much emotion as your mom does." For both Chinese and Filipino American boys, it seems that the relationship with fathers is heavily guided by prescribed gender roles.

Shared experiences. In talking about father-son relationships in the Filipino family, Filipino American boys emphasized the shared male experience, as well as joint activities between fathers and sons. As described before, boys felt their relationships with fathers were different from those with their mothers because of their gender. One Filipino boy stated, "I mean for guys it's important to be more close to your father 'cause you have a lot to relate with ... you guys are both guys." The father-son relationship is facilitated by this similarity in gender, and leads to a greater number of activities that the boys can share with their father.

Chinese American and Filipino American boys described joint activities as an important indicator of a good father-son relationship. One Chinese American boy stated, "since we're boys and guys, so we can like play sports and everything that you would do with your dad and you wouldn't usually do it with your mom." The Chinese American boys emphasized that these activities are specific to fathers; as one boy stated, "you can play sports with your dad, like basketball or, you know, but you really can't play that with your mom." Filipino American boys pointed to joint activities that are consistent with U.S. cultural stereotypes of father-son relationships (e.g., going fishing and playing sports), noting that these activities may not happen given Filipino cultural norms. One boy stated that he would like his father to take him fishing and play sports with him, but that just does not happen, no matter what he wishes. Another boy agreed and cited differences in upbringing as the reason, saying, "I think we are close but it's not the type of relationship that I would want: I'd want the fishing and the playing ball. But I mean, that's just not the way he grew up." These boys acknowledged that these joint activities are not a part of their fathers' upbringing.

You "just know" that he cares. A final prominent theme for the Chinese American boys in father-son relationships was the idea of shared understanding, consistent with girls' descriptions of "just knowing" that mothers care. Chinese American boys' communication with fathers was described as both gendered and indirect: fathers do not explicitly state that they care for sons, but it is understood. Much of the Chinese American boys' knowledge of their father's care for them was based upon acts that fathers perform, such as providing for the family financially, rather than spoken words. One boy linked his father's status as provider and enforcer to how he knows that his father cares for him, whereas another boy stated that he knows his father cares because his father tells him that he wants the best for his son. Thus, although fathers never say, "I care," they demonstrate their care and create for their sons the feeling that you "just know" that your dad cares about you. One boy stated that it is his mother who tells him that his father cares for him, supporting this idea that communication about care between fathers and sons can be through indirect means.

> Like my mom tells me all the time, like: "you know, the other night like I know he didn't want you to do this and I know you're mad, but you have to understand that your father does care about you."

Notably, although this notion of unspoken or indirect knowledge of parents' care was prominent in girls' good relationships with mothers and Chinese American boys' relationships with fathers, it was not apparent in Filipino American boys' descriptions of their relationships with fathers. Although Filipino American boys described a lack of communication that they attributed in part to Filipino culture, they were unlike the Chinese American boys because they did not directly discuss "just knowing" that fathers care.

We find that Chinese American and Filipino American boys raised similar topics when discussing relationships with mothers and fathers. In terms of maternal care, differences were apparent between the two ethnic groups in that the Chinese American boys described friendship with mothers based on the notion that mothers must establish the mother-son relationship. For Chinese American boys, there is an implicit expectation that mothers must "work" at creating this connection. For Filipino Americans, mothers' care is apparent through their direct and high levels of control, whereas for Chinese American boys, care is apparent in the number of questions the mothers ask their son about their activities. For both groups, communication was an important aspect of the father-son relationship, and both groups describe the gendered aspect of communication—that because fathers have "gone through" what they are going through, fathers are more empathetic. However, Chinese American boys see communication with fathers as relatively easy, whereas Filipino Americans suggested that communication with their fathers was limited by cultural norms. For Chinese American boys the relationship between fathers and sons is more governed by hierarchy, whereas for Filipino American boys, there is the possibility of friendship in the relationship, with descriptions of fathers as both teachers and role models.

Discussion

Our study of Chinese and Filipino American adolescents' understandings of good parent-adolescent relationships helps to illuminate prior research that identifies important ethnic group differences in parent-adolescent relationships and parenting practices. Past comparative research that has focused on ethnic differences in parent-adolescent relationships has typically compared European Americans to other ethnic groups. When the focus has been on Asians Americans, samples are typically limited to Chinese Americans. By exploring adolescents' perspectives on parent-adolescent relationships among Chinese American and Filipino American adolescent boys and girls, our work contributes to the small research literature that acknowledges the diversity among Asian Americans. Our findings are in many ways consistent with the research literature on Asian cultural characteristics of family life. At the same time we find several notable differences between Chinese and Filipino American adolescents in the ways that they describe parent-adolescent relationships.

In describing good relationships with parents, several common themes emerged in the discussions of the Chinese American and Filipina American girls: parent-daughter communication, parents' emotional closeness with daughters, and instrumental support (showing care through a mother's cooking and helping, or a father's providing). These general themes were identified in each of the focus groups with girls. Yet during the discussions the girls spent most of the time talking about how problematic these common expectations are for Asian American girls, specifically for their relationships with mothers. We have the sense that these girls are adopting the dominant model of "good parenting" or happy parent-adolescent relationships (as referenced by *The Gilmore Girls* in two of the discussions), all the while struggling to make meaning of these images in the context of family and cultural systems that are not consistent with them (Wu & Chao, 2005). Others (Fuligni, 1998) have shown that both Asian American and European American adolescents report the importance of parental closeness in doing things together and discussing problems. Our findings suggest, however, that although both Asian and European American adolescents in the United States may value parental closeness, the daily family experience of Asians may be guided by very different values or principles that are not well captured by mainstream notions of openness and emotional closeness. These girls struggle with the contradiction between dominant (U.S.) expectations of close (and even friend-like) parent-adolescent relationships and Asian family and cultural values of respect, honor, and family obligation. Wu and Chao (2005) described how these cultural discrepancies in expressions of emotional closeness and warmth between adolescents and their immigrant parents can evolve into what they label as "intergenerational cultural distance."

Several prominent themes found among Asian American girls were also evident among the boys in their discussions of good relationships with parents: boys discussed communication with parents, and gendered ways that parents show (rather than say) that they care. However, there were subtle differences in boys' descriptions of good maternal and paternal relationships. Although both Chinese American and Filipino American boys described maternal sacrifice when discussing good relationships with mothers, they differed in the maternal qualities they emphasized. The Chinese American boys described mothers' instrumental responsibilities, stressing that mothers have "maternal duties" that they must fulfill (e.g., laundry and cooking); they also described the possibility of friendship with mothers, and described mothers' questioning as a form of maternal concern and a basis for mother-son communication. In contrast, the Filipino American boys discussed affection in the mother-son relationship rather than the things that they expect mothers to do for them. They talked about trusting their mothers, a topic that was not seen in the discussions of Chinese American boys.

With regard to relationships with fathers, both Chinese American and Filipino American boys described fathers as teachers to their sons. Fathers are strong, command respect, and provide discipline. Both groups also discussed shared experiences with fathers—as teachers and providers—as the basis of a good relationship. Yet we identified ethnic differences in the ways that these experiences were interpreted. Filipino American boys talked about the possibility of fathers as teachers and role models; Chinese American boys described fathers' role as provider and teacher in terms of the respect that is expected of a son for his father.

Asian American girls "just know" that parents care based on what they do for you; Chinese American boys described relationships with their fathers in this way as well. Among these youth, open, direct communication was described as ideal, but atypical. In fact, boys clearly said that parents show that they care through their actions (maternal duties and paternal providing), and several girls talked explicitly about how their parents express their love for them by what they do for them rather than by what they say. Confucian doctrine defines good intentions as conveyed through actions more than words (Wu & Chao, 2005); these youth described parental love as being demonstrated through meeting their children's needs rather than through direct expressions of affection. Following the study in Chapter 4, it would be tempting to frame these results in terms of parental sacrifice; however, through qualitative analyses we find meanings that are more nuanced than a typical definition of "sacrifice" would imply. A growing body of research has distinguished between verbal/nonverbal and direct/indirect communication styles, demonstrating that these styles differ cross-culturally. Western cultures are more oriented toward low-context communication, in which messages are not embedded in context and verbal communication is explicit and direct. In general, Asian cultures are characterized by communication that is high-context, in which information is implied in the social context or expressed in a subtle manner. Rather than directly or explicitly stating information (as in the case of low-context communication), high-context communication relies on messages that are indirect and often nonverbal (Gudykunst, 1998; Hall, 1976). What we heard from these Asian American girls (and Chinese American boys) is clear indication that parental support and caring are expressed indirectly. In fact, their responses (e.g., "Well, it's like kind of obvious like when she makes rules and like goals for you") suggest that fulfilling the role (parent-child or familial relationship) implies that parents care for children; it does not need to be spoken. Parental sacrifice is an unspoken indication of such parental support and care.

Although others have written about the role of strictness or parental restrictions in the lives of Chinese American adolescents (Chao, 1994, 1996; Chiu, 1987), we were nevertheless struck by the degree to which the conversations among Filipino American adolescents included (and for girls seemed to be dominated by) discussions of maternal strictness or control. They stated that not only do their mothers show their love for them through instrumental care, but through setting limits and rules. Almost all references by Filipina American girls to open communication had to do with developing mutual trust and understanding so that mothers would allow more freedom; caring was discussed as a reason that mothers are strict. The prominence of strictness was notable among Filipina girls, and is consistent with Espiritu (1995, 2003), who describes Filipino parental control of daughters as rooted in the influences of Catholicism, as well as the history of prostitution associated with the U.S. military presence. These historical influences have shaped parents' roles as protecting and restricting daughters' independence. In contrast, the Chinese American girls indicated that they often do not have the freedom of typical "American" teens, yet they accept the authority of their parents. Perhaps the fundamental role of respect for and obligation to parents, central to Confucian principles and expressed by the Chinese American girls, explains why they do not interpret parental strictness as harsh, but rather as a simple fact.

Finally, our goal was to create a context in which adolescents could speak from the perspective of their ethnic group as a whole rather than from their own experience. The focus group moderators used specific strategies to help participants think from the perspective of their group while not explicitly discouraging discussions of personal family relationships. We found that the girls in our study were able to discuss relationships between mothers and daughters, while focusing on generalized mother-daughter relationships, and that this was also true for Filipina American girls in talking about fathers. Yet we found that it was particularly difficult for Chinese American girls to talk about fathers without talking about their own relationships. And although Filipina American girls generally described an emotionally open and positive relationship with fathers as difficult but possible, Chinese American girls flatly rejected the possibility of emotionally close relationships with fathers. We speculate that Chinese American girls were less able to speak abstractly about fathers and daughters because of the stark clash between their idealized model of father-daughter relationships and the realities of relationships that are based on very different principles.

References

Chao, R. K. (1994). Beyond parental control and authoritarian parenting style: Understanding Chinese parenting through the cultural notion of training. *Child Development, 65*, 1111–1119.

Chao, R. K. (1996). Chinese and European American mothers' beliefs about the role of parenting in children's school success. *Journal of Cross-Cultural Psychology, 27*, 403–423.

Chao, R. K. (2001). Extending research on the consequences of parenting style for Chinese Americans and European Americans. *Child Development, 72*, 1832–1843.

Chen, C. L., & Yang, D. C. Y. (1986). The self-image of Chinese-American adolescents: A cross-cultural comparison. *International Journal of Social Psychology*, 32, 19–26.

Chiu, L. (1987). Child-rearing attitudes of Chinese American, Chinese American-American, and European-American mothers. *International Journal of Psychology, 22*, 409–419.

Cooper, C. R., Baker, H., Polichar, D., & Welsh, M. (1993). Values and communication of Chinese, Filipino, European, Mexican, and Vietnamese American adolescents with their families and friends. *Child Development, 62*, 73–88.

Espiritu, Y. L. (1995). *Filipino American lives*. Philadelphia, PA: Temple University Press.
Espiritu, Y. L. (2003) *Home bound: Filipino American lives across cultures, communities, and countries*. Berkeley and Los Angeles, CA: University of California Press.
Fuligni, A. J. (1998). Authority, autonomy, and parent–adolescent conflict and cohesion: A study of adolescents from Mexican, Chinese, Filipino, and European backgrounds. *Developmental Psychology, 34*, 782–792.
Gudykunst, W. B. (1998). *Bridging differences: Effective intergroup communication*. Thousand Oaks, CA: Sage.
Hall, E. T. (1976). *Beyond culture*. New York: Doubleday.
Ho, D. Y. F. (1986). Chinese patterns of socialization: A critical review. In M. H. Bond (Ed.), *The psychology of the Chinese people* (pp. 1–37). Hong Kong: Oxford University.
Hsu, F. L. K. (1981). *American and Chinese: Passage to differences* (3rd ed.). Honolulu: University Press of Hawaii.
Lawton, J. T., Schuler, S. G., Fowell, N., & Madsen, M. K. (1984). Parents' perceptions of actual and ideal child-rearing practices. *The Journal of Genetic Psychology, 145*, 77–87.
LeCompte, M. D., & Schensul. J. J. (1999). *Designing and conducting ethnographic research*. Lanham, MD: AltaMira.
Miles, M. B., & Huberman, A. M. (1994). *Qualitative data analysis: A sourcebook of new methods* (2nd ed.). London: Sage Publications.
Rhee, S., Chang, J., & Rhee, J. (2003). Acculturation, communication patterns, and self-esteem among Asian and Caucasian American adolescents. *Adolescence, 38*, 749–768.
Steinberg, L. (2001). We know some things: Parent and adolescent relationships in retrospect and prospect. *Journal of Research on Adolescence, 11*, 1–19.
Wu, C. X., & Chao, R. K. (2005). Intergenerational cultural conflicts for Chinese American youth with immigrant parents: Norms of parental warmth and the consequences. *International Journal of Behavioral Development, 29*, 516–523.
Xiong, Z. B., Eliason, P. A., Detzner, D. F., & Cleveland, M. J. (2005). Southeast Asian immigrants' perceptions of good adolescents and good parents. *The Journal of Psychology, 139*, 159–175.

Chapter 6
Interdependent Independence: The Meanings of Autonomy Among Chinese American and Filipino American Adolescents

Stephen T. Russell, June Y. Chu, Lisa J. Crockett, and Sun-A Lee

The development of autonomy is said to be a primary developmental task of adolescence (Collins & Steinberg, 2006; Steinberg, 1990; Zimmer-Gembeck & Collins, 2003), yet it has been argued that this concept is derived from Western-specific perspectives of the self. The notion of an autonomous or independent self is not one that is equally shared across cultures (Markus & Kitayama, 1991). Whereas Western cultures have been described as individualistic, Asian families have been described as interdependent and collectivistic (Fuligni, 1998; Juang, Lerner, & McKinney, 1999; Yee, Huang, & Lew, 1998). Thus, in terms of parenting and the parent-adolescent relationship, the meaning and development of autonomy may differ for Asian American adolescents and families compared to European Americans. For Asian Americans, adolescent autonomy must be understood in the context of the emphasis on interdependence in the cultural history of Asian American families, as well as of processes of acculturation in the United States.

Results from prior chapters provide evidence of differences between European Americans and Asian Americans in the conceptualization of autonomy. Results from the second chapter show that the measure of autonomy-granting used in the Add Health study showed equivalence for European and Filipino American boys, but there was no indication of factorial invariance between Chinese Americans and either of the other groups. Thus, the underlying structure of autonomy-granting appears be different across these groups, and especially for Chinese Americans, at least with regard to the measure from the Add Health study. The results in Chapter 3 go further, showing that Chinese American adolescents and their parents endorse some dimensions of parental control more often than did European American adolescents and parents. Specifically, although strictness was more common among the Chinese immigrant families in the study, features of *guan* involving setting and explaining expectations and "contingent autonomy" were emphasized to a greater degree than strictness was among these families. This notion of contingent autonomy emphasizes that youth must earn their autonomy by showing they can

S.T. Russell (✉)
University of Arizona, Tucson, AZ, USA
e-mail: strussell@arizona.edu

S.T. Russell et al. (eds.), *Asian American Parenting and Parent-Adolescent Relationships*, Advancing Responsible Adolescent Development,
DOI 10.1007/978-1-4419-5728-3_6, © Springer Science+Business Media, LLC 2010

act responsibly. This work suggests that the experiences of autonomy, or meanings associated with the concept, are grounded in Asian cultural expectations of collectivism, particularly familial obligations. Together the results from Chapter 2 and Chapter 3 suggest that Chinese (and to some extent Filipino) American adolescents may understand autonomy in ways that are distinct from individualist notions of "independence" from parents.

Following the discussions of good parent-adolescent relationships and parental support in the focus group interviews described in the prior chapter, the moderator stated: "Now we'd like to ask you about autonomy, or making your own decisions independently. For Chinese American [Filipino] American teens, what does it mean to be independent and make your own decisions?" Discussion typically began with exchanges about the definitions of autonomy and independence. Two follow-up probes were used by the moderator to encourage further discussion, "How would teens describe being independent? What do parents think about teens making their own decisions?"

Results

In describing autonomy in relation to their parents, the Asian American adolescents we interviewed, particularly the boys, provided definitions of adolescent independence that would be considered typical for Western youth. However, these definitions were followed by in-depth discussions of the interdependent nature of independence: girls described autonomy in relational terms, and boys in contingent or negotiated terms. Girls consistently defined independence in reference to their relationships with parents. For girls, parents often "know best," but this theme differed somewhat for Chinese American and Filipina American girls. For girls in both groups, parents know best and therefore limit girls' autonomous decision-making about long-term life choices; however, limit setting focused on college decisions for Chinese American girls and on general life goals for Filipino American girls. Girls seem to adopt their parents' agendas for their behavior as their own, and consequently made their decisions within the boundaries of their parents' preferences. Although boys described an interdependent independence as well, theirs was a negotiated autonomy based on respect and empathy for parents. Finally, we point out ethnic differences in access to and expectations about autonomy: Filipino American adolescents described their parents as ultimately wanting their children to become autonomous and independent, whereas Chinese American adolescents indicated that for them independence came about in situations in which their immigrant parents lacked experience and information about the lives and life choices of adolescents in the United States.

Gendered Definitions of Autonomy and Independence

Boys. Asian American boys provided detailed descriptions of the multiple meanings or dimensions of independence. In their definitions of autonomy, both Chinese

American and Filipino American boys described the importance of making one's own decisions and being able to live without your parents. Regarding decision making, Chinese American boys gave examples of deciding what music to listen to ("me and my sister kind of like made it so every time we're in the car we can listen to the radio instead of listening to like Chinese American CDs"), whether or not to do homework, or even whether or not to get into or walk away from a fight at school. One Chinese American boy described autonomy as: "deciding what college you want to go to, 'cause some teens, their parents pick the college for them ... I think picking your own college is a big decision, like the first big decision that you would make in your life." Additionally, taking responsibility was identified as an important dimension of independence. For instance, one Chinese American boy talked about his financial debts, and how autonomy involves taking care of these on his own without asking for parental assistance:

> I have never told my parents how much I owed for any of these things because I feel that I have done this [on] my own—I bought all these things, I played all these games, I should be the one taking care of it. I feel that ... I did it on my own so I need to take care of it on my own without putting the burden on them ....

This boy construed taking responsibility for his debts as independence, noting empathy for his parents as a partial motive for his desire to take responsibility. Autonomy also was described as living on one's own or without one's parents. One Filipino boy said, "you don't really need the support of your parents anymore. Like you'll be able to make it on your own and you don't need to ask your parents for help and ask them to take care of your problems." Similarly, a Chinese American boy put it this way:

> Where you can like go out into the public and survive on your own, not coming back to your parents and saying, "Oh, can you help me with this, can you support me with that?" Well, that's independence. ... If you can go out and then handle all the stuff out there by yourself.

One Chinese American boy described independence in terms of self-reliance: "... you're constantly not dependent on your parents. It's like you're more like relying on yourself ...."
Chinese American boys also described "living without parents" in ways that suggested it was a future, adult-like status, rather than one that was immediately accessible to adolescents. One Chinese American boy put it this way:

> To be independent is to mainly live without your parents and without their permission to do anything as in getting a tattoo, go out and shopping anytime you want, and just spending the money you want to. The way you keep your lifestyle, the way you dress, or anything without saying—without asking your parents, "Can I do this? Can I wear that? Can I go there?"

For this boy, "living without your parents" was not defined as being self-reliant but as freedom from having to ask permission to engage in activities and behaviors that are viewed as everyday or lifestyle choices.

Financial independence was described specifically by Filipino American (but not Chinese American) boys as one way in which they demonstrate autonomy.

Filipino American boys talked about being able to buy your food, pay your bills, and maintain a roof over your head as important to becoming independent.

Girls. When asked what it means to be autonomous, Filipina Americans provided multi-dimensional definitions of autonomy. When first asked what things they are able to make decisions about, one girl answered: "I think as a teen you can make your own decisions ... in your surroundings. Sort of like who your friends are, like what classes you want to take ...." She went on to say "but you have to get that approval from your parents" about things that are "reality," related to school, education, and life plans. This girl distinguished different domains of decision making (everyday decisions versus life choices), some of which afford opportunities for autonomy. However, the Filipina Americans generally described independence in interdependent terms:

> I think they [decisions] should be satisfying to your parents but like not so much like it's something that you don't want to do. I mean, because that's why they say they want you to know from good from bad. You make your decision not to do drugs and that's a good thing 'cause you don't want to get into that, but like other things like materialistic kind of things like oh ... I want it now and that kind of thing and your parents, they have to say no, you didn't earn it. ... I guess it's decisions to do good things that you won't get in trouble for.

For this girl, independent decisions are defined as those that are positive moral choices that are acceptable to both parents and the adolescent. Another Filipina American said,

> I think my parents sort of allow me and my sister to make our own decisions like when are we going to sleep or where we're going to go. But then they have to know first. Like they just want to be kind of over everything we do and I think that that shows that they really love us ... they trust us of what we know is good and bad because they raised us that way. And I just think if we do something bad, we know, we have that conscience in our head that our parents don't want us to do it so I think we grow into individuals that way.

Here interdependent independence is explicit: a daughter can make her own everyday decisions, as long as parents know about and approve of it in advance. Further, an adolescent's decisions are influenced by her conscience, based on values that are internalized from her parents. This girl described an internalization of parental rules (Goodnow & Grusec, 1994) consistent with the Asian cultural value of behaving in ways that support group harmony rather than in ways that express personal desires (Markus & Kitayama, 1991).

For Chinese American girls, independence is fundamentally defined in relation to the family unit. Chinese American girls suggested that "being allowed to make your own decisions" and "having your own options to do things" contribute to a sense of autonomy. However, they described independence in terms of the obligations implicit in their family roles (specifically as daughters in relation to parents). Although these girls said that they were independent and making their own choices, this independence was understood in the context of obeying or being responsible to their parents. Autonomy meant choosing decisions and actions that were expected based on a daughter's role within the family:

> I think for me, like I think being the oldest, just the first-born child, just gives me autonomy, like independence, like the decisions I make or the way I look over my sisters or like the responsibilities I choose to take on myself.

This Chinese American girl stated that her autonomy comes from her status as an older, first-born child, who had responsibility for looking over siblings and taking on family chores. She made decisions within the boundaries of her role obligations, which underscores the relational aspect of independence. Another Chinese American girl discussed how she was free to stay out late in the evenings, a sign of independence. However, she saw it as her responsibility as an independent person to call her parents and touch base:

> I was up a week with my best friend. And even when they weren't home I felt like I needed to—I should call back even though they really—they knew I was fine—I'd still call back and tell them what I did for the day or something. In a way that's independent of me to choose to do that.

This girl defined independence explicitly in terms of her felt obligation to communicate with her parents: calling home is not a burden or family rule, rather her action is understood as a choice showing independence.

Asian American Girls: Parents Know Best

In talking about independence, the Chinese American girls described the idea that parents know what is best for them:

> Well, for me, like my parents, they don't want me to be independent when I'm young because they say I don't know what I'm thinking yet, I'm still young, I don't know what I want and I'm just going to regret it for the rest of my life. And so in the beginning, like they made me go to a private high school but then I think about it and I really hated that they were making decisions for me. But I was thinking maybe in the long run they might be right. I'm probably going to realize that later but maybe like I would have fell for the peer pressure and they probably knew that I'd fall for a lot of peer pressure and that I don't know what I'm doing right now. So maybe it was a good thing that they made decisions for me.

This Chinese American girl seemed to accept the limits her parents placed on her autonomy, arguing that it is a good thing. In contrast, another Chinese American adolescent described the interdependent character of independence as parental over-protection:

> I think for me like mostly my mom ... she trusts me to do the things that I like want to do but she's I think really cautious and over-protective like a lot of the time. So when I want to make a decision I always think oh, you know, should I ask my mom just in case ... for me I feel like I have to ask her sometimes, you know. And ... she doesn't like to make my decisions for me either.

This girl described her mother as over-protective, and while she argued that her mother does not make decisions for her, it is clear that her decisions are made in reference to her mother's caution. Thus, parents are seen as wanting to make decisions for their children to protect them from making mistakes, and Chinese mothers are described as especially cautious and over-protective. Another Chinese American girl explained that parents are scared that daughters will make the wrong decisions:

> I think that they're scared for us because I guess it's still the beginning, like we still depend on them, like one way or another. And so like they've raised us for however many years that we are right now and ... after all that they've done for us, they don't want us just to like mess up our lives with the wrong decisions. So I guess that's why they're scared.

This girl empathized with parents, she accepted that parents fear that their children will make "wrong decisions," and offered this as a rationale for parental restriction of adolescent autonomy.

According to Filipina Americans, Filipino American parents helped children with decisions and attempt to restrict autonomy seeking as a means of protecting children:

> I think they would rather not let us make like our decisions for us .... I mean, I know she trusts like when she tells me stuff, she tries to guide me in a good way, but I'm here like pulling back and I kinda just want to do my own thing so it kinda scares her, I guess, 'cause she's afraid that I'll make mistakes and they'll like put me on the bad side.

This Filipina American seemed to empathize with her mother's concerns. However, she was explicit in saying that she was "pulling back," and wanting to "do my own thing." Another Filipino American girl elaborated on this idea of protection, suggesting that parents restrict decision-making to help girls avoid bad decisions:

> If you have a parent that doesn't care what you wear, if you wear like slutty clothing, then you're going to be seen as like a whore and if you wear formal, I mean, not formal but presentable clothing that's respectable for everyone to be okay with, it shows that your parents do care that you're not being just out there in the world just showing off or whatever.

For this girl, maternal caring was linked to public expectations and, presumably, to concern with the ways that individual behavior becomes a reflection on one's family.

For Chinese American girls, the first specific topic that came up in the discussions about independent decision-making among both groups had to do with college. Girls provided examples of ways that Chinese American parents restricted the college choices of their children. For example,

> ... a lot of my Chinese American friends, their parents are forcing them to go into a certain major, a certain study, a certain school. And to me that's disheartening because they would want to do something else but their parents say no, you have to be a pharmacist or you've got to be, you know, an eye doctor.

Several Chinese American girls described their college decisions as independent, but at the same time indicated that parents had closely guided the decision, or set parameters for or limits around their college possibilities. For example, one girl said,

> In the beginning ... it was UCs [University of California campuses] and then actually I finally convinced them in a way, 'cause they're learning and everything so they're like oh, you know, maybe UC is not the best for you ... And like for my mom, she really wants me to go to a school in California so actually all the schools I applied to were in California. But I didn't take it in a sense that it was a lack of independence because I like my family, I like staying here. I mean, being in California, it doesn't bother me and I don't mind going—I don't mind staying close to home. I have my own little niche. So it wasn't a bother.

This participant defined her college choices as her own. However, her parents exerted an influence in her college choice, because she chose to apply only to colleges that are located in California. She described this as an autonomous decision about college while recognizing her parents' wishes and adhering to their preference. Another Chinese American girl discussed parental involvement in college decisions in a lighthearted manner:

> Well, I know my parents are like, they want to make all my decisions for me, but they have to understand that there's a point where they have to stop. And I think that's when I enter college . . . I had a conversation with my sister and my mom once and me and my sister were just joking around. We were like: "Choose my major, mommy, choose mine." And she was like: "I did. You're going to be a doctor, you're going to be a lawyer." We're like: "okay." We just laughed because we know we can make our own [choices], but . . . she thinks she knows what's the best for us kids but . . . she can't make decisions for us forever.

While Filipino American adolescent girls did not focus on college per se, they did indicate that parents generally did not allow children to make their own decisions, particularly about major life plans or goals:

> Like I wanted to be a beautician but they said no, you're not going to do that 'cause we're not going to let you. And like no daughter of mine is going to do something—'cause that's not realizing your full potential. And that showed me that they care but I'm not going to be happy, you know. Like I want to be a history teacher also, but then my mom still has something to say about that. Like she says you're not going to make any money, you're not going to be happy . . . . Like they didn't go to college but they still succeeded, but they think that they can tell me what to do but they haven't experienced it yet, so they don't let me make my own decisions like with my education.

This participant did not appear to accept her mother's opinion about her career or life goals as readily as the Chinese American girls did. Rather than describing autonomous decisions that are based on parents' preferences, Filipino American girls perceived a lack of autonomy in important life decisions. Another participant said, "most of the Filipino American parents I know don't really let their kids make their own goals. Like they tell you what to be." This participant started off discussing how Filipino American parents do not let children set their life goals independently; she goes on to talk about school grades:

> But I think one way that my parents are . . . allowing me to make my own decisions lately is like my grades. Like before, if I were to get a C, I would get my ass whooped. But like they just saw my semester report card and I was afraid to show it to them 'cause I had like a D, Cs and I failed French, and it's very important for them, like grades are very important. But they saw the report card and my mom's just, "These are ugly grades" and she just put it down. And she said, "If you want to go to college then you know you can't get into college with these grades." And that's all she said. I mean, I think that's better too because when they nag me it's just like man, shut up, stop talking, stop, oh! Like that's all I'm thinking in my head. But when my mom said that, it really made me think.

These statements suggest that there are different domains of independence: to this girl, Filipino American parents do not let adolescents make life goal decisions (like "what to be"), but allow them to make intermediate decisions about things such as school work.

Asian American Boys and Contingent Autonomy

While Asian American girls described an interdependent independence in relation to their parents, we characterize the boys' descriptions as negotiated or contingent autonomy (Chao, 2005); they describe ways that parents continue to be there to provide support as boys develop independence. One Chinese American boy acknowledged the advising role parents can play: "at some points in time you need to ask your parents because sometimes they do know more about these situations." A Filipino American boy spoke of the importance of parental figures in their lives, "You can decide on like what you want to do and like your life, but then you could also have your mother or parents [give] advice to help you get there." A Chinese American boy described independence coming from parents' trust in the adolescents' decision-making abilities: "being able to make these decisions kind of means that your parents are okay with you making your own decisions because most likely they know what kind of person you are and how you would make these decisions." In this case, the implication was that parents will allow sons to make their own decisions if they can trust their decision-making capabilities, similar to Chao's (2005) notion of contingent autonomy. Thus, although many of the boys stated that independence is being able to make decisions on your own, they also saw parents as important resources as they become independent: "You can always ask your parents for advice or you should ask your parents for permission, but in the end, you're making the final choice and that final choice is independence right there" (Chinese American boy).

When asked what parents thought about their children making their own decisions, Asian American boys described tension between children and parents as parents begin to "let go." One Filipino American boy claimed that at first, his parents felt as if their "baby" was growing up, but that parents respect children's autonomous behavior:

> I think ... over a period of time 'cause like when it first starts to happen 'its like, "Oh my baby's growing up." Then you're like—you start leaving on them. And in the end they're going to learn to respect that. They did their job to raise you to be able to do all that and they're going to understand.

The boys believe that as you get older, parents will want you to make your own decisions, but if you are young, they will be reluctant to grant autonomy. This is particularly so if you continue to live in our parent's home, where children remain under their parent's control: "... you're still living under their control, under their power, and you can't just make decisions on your own without their consent" (Filipino American boy).

One Chinese American boy described the negotiation of independence between adolescents and their Chinese American parents as difficult for parents, and attributed this tension to Chinese American culture.

> I guess it's like—it offends them, to me, 'cause Chinese American parents, you tend to—like they raise their child to be like close to them, close to the family, and they want them to be ... high achievers and always stay close with family .... And then once the child starts,

> you know, getting his or her own job, doing what she wants to do on Friday nights or school nights or weekend nights, week days ... it kind of like hurts them because you're kind of leaving away from them and I guess Chinese American parents they have a really strong bond with their sons and daughters.

This boy described a built-in tension for Chinese American families as they negotiate adolescent independence. Children must maintain close relationships and honor parental authority, but they desire the personal autonomy that they see as typical for contemporary teenagers. One Chinese American boy pointed out that these challenges are not unique, however, to Asian Americans:

> Well, maybe it's not just us Chinese Americans, but then like if I was a parent and like all my life, like I raised my children, and then like they used to talk to me when they were young. And then like now when they're growing up, like especially during their teens years, they start like doing stuff on their own, I don't know about it, or if they won't like tell me about it, then I would feel like the bond's breaking apart.

This boy acknowledged that the negotiation that characterizes the parent-adolescent relationship in Chinese American families may not be culturally specific.

We note that respect for parents and understanding parents' perspectives and roles are central to understandings of autonomy and independence for the Asian American boys. One Chinese American boy said, "If I want to go somewhere, I mean I tell them but it doesn't mean that I wouldn't really think twice about doing it if I know I'm going to do it or if there's something I want to do." Thus, while independent decision making is central to autonomy, this boy acknowledged that he felt a responsibility to tell his parents about decisions he makes. Independence involves a sense of interdependence—of consideration for parents: "I go out and I might not be home until like 4:00 or so, but I still tell my parents. They might not like it but I at least tell them so they worry less about me" (Chinese American boy).

The Asian American boys we interviewed have empathy for parents, recognizing that as adolescents seek independence it may make parents feel that their bond with the child is being broken. While they can clearly identify the meaning of autonomy or independence, they also remain aware of the relationship that is directly affected by teenagers' expressions of personal autonomy and seek to alleviate some parental worries. In this sense, autonomy is exercised and negotiated contingently, in a way that maintains respect for and sensitivity to parents.

Filipino American Parents Want Sons' and Daughters' Independence

A notable difference between the Chinese American and Filipino American adolescents' discussions of independence was that Filipino American adolescents indicated that their parents ultimately want them to be independent; this sentiment was not expressed in discussions among the Chinese American adolescents. According to one Filipino American boy, children's eventual independence is a goal of child rearing,

> Well, I think—I mean being like a parenting thing when you raise your child you want them to be independent . . . . I think they think it's good if it gets to the point where . . . you know that your parents figure you're independent when . . . they don't need to tell you to do things like 'cause you know how—you know when to do it on your own and—you know how to do your own chores . . . they don't have to always get on your case.

Here autonomy is defined as responsible, independent fulfillment of one's duties in the family. Although a goal of Filipino child rearing may be to create children who can be independent, parents are obligated to take care of their children and keep them from harm if they may potentially make a wrong choice:

> Being independent is making your own decisions as long as you're willing to live with the consequences, good or bad. I think parents should be able to be supportive of how their teens decide, but at the same time not be afraid to put their foot in the door if it's potentially hurting them or if they have a different opinion. That's their right and it's their obligation to inform the teen. (Filipino American boy)

The Filipino American boys also believed that while it is important for parents to let their children learn on their own, parents should remain a part of their lives as teachers:

> I think parents should like . . . let the child like go freely and independent . . . but they should never restrict anything of the learning process. They should always be teaching them . . . this could be wrong, that can be right. But they should never say this is always wrong, you should never do this, I don't think you should do this . . . .

For this boy, Filipino American parents should continue to advise and teach their adolescent children, but in ways that acknowledge the adolescents' ultimate autonomy.

Filipina Americans also described independence as something that Filipino American parents want. One girl discussed how her father supports her autonomy:

> I think in general that my parents allow me to be autonomous I guess. Like even though my dad is like conservative and he's not into activism and stuff like that, he allows me to do this and I guess like it's just that they want me to be able to form my own opinions and they have a lot of problems with like people who just tell their kids what to think. And so my dad will tell me about his experiences and by allowing me to have my own experiences, like he just shows that—I don't know how to put it into words. Like that he just wants me to form my own opinions and that he wants me to make my own decisions and be independent.

She finished, however, by citing the difference between her parents: "But I think it's opposite with my mom 'cause my mom was raised more out in like a more traditional Filipino American family, where she'll just tell me what to think." For this participant, her father promotes (or allows) free thinking and independence, whereas her mother restricts it. Other participants discussed how parents want their daughters to learn to be financially independent: "My parents, they want me to be independent by instead of depending on them for money or for my finances, that I'd have to work and finance myself that way, like make my own income that way instead of depending on them." A second girl said, "My parents like—the autonomous word, I guess yeah, being able to like I guess fend for your own things like . . . clothes, instead of asking your parents for money all the time." These Filipino American parents encourage their daughters to make their own money and be somewhat financially independent.

One Filipina American girl was unusual in describing parental leniency and autonomy-granting:

> Actually, my parents are like really lenient. They give me a lot of freedom . . . For example, college, my career, banking, wherever I go. But they also expect me to . . . set my own limits. They guide me but they want me to make my own limits.

In this case, parents may allow independent decision-making within reasonable limits; from this girl's perspective, parents expect adolescents to define and set their own limits. These were atypical statements, but are important because they illustrate the notions of parental guidance and expectations that the adolescent will "set limits" and make good choices.

Chinese American Parents and Adolescent Autonomy

Finally, the Chinese American adolescents discussed ways that they were more independent than their parents desired due to their parents' immigration and childhood outside the United States. In some situations the Chinese American boys saw themselves as more knowledgeable than parents, and because of this, they have more independence:

> 'Cause we grew up going to school—we grew up learning English. They are there at home working, whatever, and they don't know it. And it's also like you're out in the world. You know what's going on. You've lived here almost all your life. . . . Even though they might have lived here longer than you have, they're in their own little world working, taking care of the family, and all that. And they like watch the news and everything but they only see the bad parts of the world. They don't—they see all the crimes, all the homicides, killing, war, all these things. But they don't really know what's going on at—it might be safe where you are but they just don't know.

Several Chinese American boys mentioned unintentional independence with regard to education and school decisions, "like the major—the college thing. I have made my own decisions because I think I know more than my parents 'cause I gain a lot of information that they don't, and the college is for me and not them." Finally, one boy pointed out that while adolescents sometimes have knowledge that allows independence, parents still deserve respect: "It's true you are in America longer, you do know more things but they are older than you and so they are wiser even if they haven't been in America as long as you. They still know certain things." Although this participant acknowledged that parents still know more than their children, the participants generally agreed that Chinese American parents remain "out of touch" with how mainstream U.S. culture operates.

Like the boys, some Chinese American girls cited parent-adolescent differences in information and resources relevant to U.S. higher education as a basis for their independence in this domain. One girl said:

> Well, I mean, 'cause the thing is like both of them came from China ... and so they don't really know a lot about what courses I should take or anything so maybe that's why I have a say in what I want to take, what classes I want to take, and where I want to go when I grow up, college and stuff, but that's about it.

For this girl and other Chinese American adolescents with immigrant parents, college decisions were the primary area in which she felt she could make independent decisions.

Discussion

In describing autonomy, each group provided typical definitions of adolescent independence, but also discussed the interdependent nature of independence. These Asian American youth defined independence in reference to their relationships with parents, and in relational and contingent terms. For girls, independence is interdependent due to mutually understood family role obligations: parents know what is best for their daughters, and daughters express autonomy by making choices consistent with their parent's preferences. For Chinese American girls, parents' role pertained to choices about college, and parents' lower levels of acculturation were discussed as explanations for parental perspectives on independence. Some parents of Filipino American girls wanted them to be autonomous; girls distinguished between decisions about life goals versus day-to-day decisions, about which their parents allowed more independence. For boys, consistent with the notion of contingent autonomy (Chao, 2005), autonomy was negotiated with parents. Being independent meant to live on your own, but further discussion revealed the degree to which this independence was negotiated with parents and expressed with sensitivity to parental concerns.

Prior research on Asian American parenting and parent-adolescent relationships has been dominated by studies of Chinese American families. Due to the emphasis on Chinese Americans and Chinese culture, there is a risk of incorrectly attributing dimensions of Chinese culture to all Asian Americans. The understandings of autonomy expressed by Filipino American adolescents in our study extend current thinking about "Asian American" parenting. We found that although parental negotiations and approval were central to adolescent girls' ideas of personal autonomy, the Filipina Americans seemed to desire and to feel entitled to more independence than Chinese American girls, at least in everyday decisions, but did not feel that they had independence in setting life goals. Thus, interdependent independence takes a somewhat different form in the two ethnic groups. Whereas the Filipina Americans began the discussion of independence with behaviors that signal autonomy, the Chinese American girls first began by stating that they are not allowed to be very independent. For some of the Chinese American girls, it seemed that autonomy was not something that parents willingly handed to them, but rather was a consequence of their parents' immigrant status: they have autonomy by virtue of the circumstances of immigration. Because some immigrant parents did not have the information or experiences with U.S. educational systems, for example, some Chinese American girls have autonomy in areas (e.g., schooling) that they may not have had otherwise. Compared to Filipina American girls, Chinese American girls seemed to attribute greater wisdom to their parents and showed greater acceptance of parents making decisions for them. They adopted their parents' perspective as their own and make "independent" decisions within the parameters set by parental expectations and preferences.

The Chinese American girls discussed parental authority with the caveat that their parents most likely do know what is best for them and should therefore be part of the decision-making process. They described their parents as over-protecting; notably, Chinese American boys used over-protection to describe maternal support—or "just knowing" that mothers care. Filipino American adolescents emphasized financial independence in their descriptions of decision making and independence. Their emphasis on financial independence may be rooted in Western cultural values of independence and self-sufficiency. In addition, instrumental support among family members has long been a prominent value of Filipino American families. Indeed, some studies have indicated that Filipino American young adults are more likely than other East Asian young adults to endorse providing future material help to their families (Fuligni & Pedersen, 2002). Other work indicates that Filipino American children are expected to provide for the basic needs of the family, such as tuition for siblings' schooling (Dubrow, Pena, Masten, Sesma, & Williamson, 2001). Filipino American adolescents' emphasis on financial independence may be best understood as a combination of Western values and Filipino American familial values.

Decisions about college (choices of college and courses of study) were central in focus group discussions with Chinese American adolescents, but not in discussions with Filipino American adolescents (although college was briefly mentioned by Filipino American girls as an arena for independent decision-making). Chinese American girls described parents' influence regarding college choices, and Chinese American boys discussed the college decision as an example of contingent autonomy. The unique role of and value for education among Asian Americans (Caplan, Whitmore, & Choy, 1989; Julian, McHenry, & McKelvey, 1994; Yao, 1985) may be important here, but it is unclear why this cultural value would be distinct for Chinese American compared to Filipino American youth. Ours is not a large sample, but it is notable that even though the focus groups were conducted within the same communities (urban as well as suburban) for each ethnic group, this distinction seemed pronounced.

Whereas girls' view of parents' role in their independence was that they know best, boys' perspective was that parents play an advising role—one that deserves sons' respect. Thus, the tenor of interdependent independence differs for boys and girls, but was evident for both. When boys talked about autonomy in their real lives, they revealed that their autonomy or independent decision-making should be enacted while showing respect to their parents. This does not necessarily mean that they want or follow parental authority in their decision-making. Rather, they make decisions based on parental advice, and they often inform their parents, but do not necessarily follow their parents' preferences as do girls; they do not want to make parents worry about their behaviors or feel offended by those independent behaviors. In short, Asian American teenagers understand and describe autonomy in ways that are consistent with dominant Western ideas of autonomy, and at the same time the independent decision-making or autonomous behaviors that they describe are made in reference to, or involve, their parents. Rather than interpreting parents' behaviors as controlling, Chinese American adolescents may view them as expectations of filial obligation (see Gorman, 1998, for a discussion of Chinese American mothers' attitudes about parenting and parental expectations for their adolescent children).

The differences between Chinese American and Filipino American adolescents in "interdependent independence" can be understood in the context of historical cultural group differences. Chinese American family values are heavily rooted in Confucianism, and these values have provided a basis upon which parent-child relationships are developed in China. According to Ho (1994), a Confucian foundation supports the collectivistic values of the culture, which stress the importance of obligations to others rather than the rights of each individual family member. Chinese American families are also influenced by the Confucian values of hierarchical relationships, respect for authority, and filial piety. In contrast, Filipino Americans have been influenced by Catholicism and Spanish history and culture, both of which have their roots in the individualistic models of relationships. The colonization of the Philippines by Americans and the adoption of the English language in 1898 led to the incorporation of American cultural values. Perhaps for these reasons, Filipino American families are more likely to be egalitarian than patriarchal (Agbayani-Siewert, 1994) when compared to other Asian ethnic groups. Nevertheless, Filipino American families also are described as interdependent, family members depend upon each other for support, and binding relationships are created through reciprocal obligations, referred to as *utang ng loob* (Agbayani-Siewert, 1994).

Chao (1994) and McDermott (2001) have argued that Chinese American culture is based on Confucian doctrines in which goals for individuals focus on the value of harmony for the group. This value extends to the individual's respect for elders. One teen in our study said, "to be independent is, for me . . . I feel I shouldn't put the burden on my parents" (Chinese American boy). We may understand this "burden" to parents as an awareness that family members, especially children, are expected to satisfy family honor or meet parental expectation. When a member of a family does not meet family expectations, he or she shames the family. The adolescents in our study place a great deal of emphasis on accountability and responsibility in their discussions of autonomy; to be independent is to be responsible for oneself while considering parents' wishes and perspectives.

In summary, prior research, and the empirical studies presented in the second and third chapters, suggests culturally based differences in the meanings of independence and autonomy for Asian American adolescents and families. Results of this chapter support the findings of prior quantitative research, and add richness to our understandings of autonomy for Asian American adolescents. This study highlights the distinct Asian cultural basis that provides the context of autonomy-granting in Asian American families, and shows the ways that independence differs among Asian Americans based on adolescents' gender, for mothers versus fathers, and based on ethnicity.

References

Agbayani-Siewert, P. (1994). Filipino American culture and family: Guidelines for practitioners. *Families in Society, 75*, 429–438.

Caplan, N., Whitmore, J. K., & Choy, M. H. (1989). *The boat people and achievement in America: A study of family life, hard work, and cultural values*. Ann Arbor: University of Michigan Press.

Chao, R. K. (1994). Beyond parental control and authoritarian parenting style: Understanding Chinese parenting through the cultural notion of training. *Child Development, 65*, 1111–1119.

Chao, R. K. (2005). *The importance of Guan in describing the parental control of immigrant Chinese American*. Unpublished manuscript, University of California at Riverside.

Collins, W. A., & Steinberg, L. (2006). Adolescent development in interpersonal context. In N. Eisenberg, W. Damon, & R. M. Lerner (Eds.), *Handbook of child psychology: Vol. 3. Social, emotional, and personality development* (6th ed., pp. 1003–1067). Hoboken, NJ: John Wiley & Sons Inc.

Durbrow, E. H., Pena, L. F., Masten, A., Sesma, A., & Williamson, I. (2001). Mothers' conceptions of child competence in contexts of poverty: The Philippines, St. Vincent, and the United States. *International Journal of Behavioral Development, 25*, 438–443.

Fuligni, A. J. (1998). Authority, autonomy, and parent–adolescent conflict and cohesion: A study of adolescents from Mexican, Chinese, Filipino, and European backgrounds. *Developmental Psychology, 34*, 782–792.

Fuligni, A. J., & Pedersen, S. (2002). Family obligation and the transition to young adulthood. *Developmental Psychology, 38*, 856–868.

Goodnow, J. J., & Grusec, J. E. (1994). Impact of parental discipline methods on the child's internalization of values. *Developmental Psychology, 30*, 4–19.

Gorman, J. C. (1998). Parenting attitudes and practices of immigrant Chinese American mothers of adolescents. *Family Relations, 47*, 73–80.

Ho, D. Y. F. (1994). Cognitive socialization in Confucian heritage cultures. In P. M. Greenfield and R. R. Cocking (Eds.), *Cross-cultural roots of minority child development* (pp. 285–313). Hillsdale, NJ: Erlbaum.

Juang, L. P., Lerner, J. V., & McKinney, J. P. (1999). The goodness of fit in autonomy timetable expectations between Asian-American late adolescents and their parents. *International Journal of Behavioral Development, 23*, 1023–1048.

Julian, T. W., McHenry, P. C., & McKelvey, M. W. (1994). Cultural variations in parenting, perceptions of Caucasian, African American, Hispanic, and Asian American parents. *Family Relations, 43*, 30–37.

Markus, H. R., & Kitayama, S. (1991). Culture and the self: Implications for cognition, emotion, and motivation. *Psychological Review, 98*, 224–253.

McDermott, J. (2001). Chinese history: A manual, revised and enlarged [Review of the book *Chinese history: A manual, revised and enlarged*]. *Journal of Asian Studies, 60*, 192–194.

Steinberg, L. (1990). Interdependence in the family: Autonomy, conflict, and harmony in the parent–adolescent relationship. In S. S. Feldman & G. L. Elliott (Eds.), *At the threshold: The developing adolescent* (pp. 255–276). Cambridge, MA: Harvard University Press.

Yao, E. L. (1985). Adjustment needs of Asian immigrant children. *Elementary School Guidance & Counseling, 19*, 222–227.

Yee, B. W. K., Huang, L. N., & Lew, A. (1998). Families: Life-span socialization in a cultural context. In L. C. Lee & N. W. S. Zane (Eds.), *Handbook of Asian American psychology* (pp. 83–135). Thousand Oaks, CA: Sage.

Zimmer-Gembeck, M. J., & Collins, W. A. (2003). Autonomy development during adolescence. In G. R. Adams & M. D. Berzonsky (Eds.), *Blackwell handbook of adolescence* (pp. 175–204). Malden, MA: Blackwell Publishing.

Chapter 7
Conclusions: The Role of Asian American Culture in Parenting and Parent-Adolescent Relationships

Stephen T. Russell, Lisa J. Crockett, and Ruth K. Chao

We have shown in this book that ideas about parenting and family relationships are rooted in culture. We argue that "mainstream" thinking about parenting and parent-child relationships is grounded in Western cultural assumptions, beliefs, and practices regarding parenting and family life. These assumptions and beliefs are reflected and reinforced everyday—through daily family interactions, but also through popular media and cultural representations of families. These images tell us what it means to be parents, and what adolescents and their relationships with their parents are *supposed to be* like.

Scientific research on adolescence, parenting, and family life has been conducted alongside these dominant cultural ideas. As both a product and contributor to that culture, science has reinforced many of the ideas that have become part of the collective understanding of what is believed to be fundamental to family relationships. Historically typical approaches to the study of parenting—the choices of samples, methods, and measures—reflect dominant Western thinking about parents and adolescents. That is, Western ways of thinking about contemporary families are dominant among researchers, as well as among parents and adolescents themselves. These conceptualizations of family and parenting have been the basis of (and derived from) studies of European Americans (or, in the case of Asian Americans, samples have been largely limited to Chinese Americans). Too often prior research has been based on assumptions that there is conceptual similarity in the meanings of fundamental dimensions of parenting (parental support or warmth and control) across cultures. Most of the research in this field has been based in the United States and has been conducted through studies of European American families. Such thinking obscures cultural differences in expectations about and understandings of parent-adolescent relationships.

Using multiple methodological and analytic strategies, this unique set of studies has highlighted differences between European, Chinese, and Filipino Americans, the two largest Asian American ethnic groups in the United States. Our quantitative

S.T. Russell (✉)
University of Arizona, Tucson, AZ, USA
e-mail: strussell@arizona.edu

S.T. Russell et al. (eds.), *Asian American Parenting and Parent-Adolescent Relationships*, Advancing Responsible Adolescent Development,
DOI 10.1007/978-1-4419-5728-3_7,

analyses of surveys from adolescents and parents and qualitative analysis of adolescents' perceptions of parental support and control show that understandings of parenting vary by ethnicity, as well as by adolescent and parent gender.

Our purpose is not to suggest that Asian American parenting is fundamentally different from European American parenting; many of our results for Asian American families are relevant for all families. However, we suggest that the combination of across and within ethnic group analyses presented here highlights culturally distinct dimensions of parenting and parent-adolescent relationships among Asian Americans. These distinctions have historically been absent from models and conceptualizations of parenting. By bringing these cultural distinctions to light, more can be learned not only about the parenting and family relationships of Asian Americans but, more importantly, about how well our theories and conceptualizations of parenting and family relationships fit current populations of youth and their families in the United States. Our results allow us to highlight the variability in family and cultural processes beyond that which has been represented in Western cultures and Western research on families and parenting.

In this chapter we synthesize the key findings we have presented. We then acknowledge the limitations of these studies and point to avenues for future research that may be particularly fruitful. Parent-adolescent relationships and parenting strategies are undoubtedly crucial for child and adolescent adjustment; we close with a consideration of the implications of this work for future studies of adolescent adjustment. Our work suggests the need for continued attention to the ways that ethnicity and culture shape human development through family relationships.

The Cultural Basis of Asian American Parenting

Our analyses focus on two dimensions that have been central to the literature on parent-adolescent relationships and parenting: warmth and support, and autonomy-granting and independence. We consider the implications of our studies for each dimension below, highlighting cultural distinctions that characterize Asian American parent-adolescent relationships and parenting, as well as the differences between Chinese and Filipino Americans.

Understanding Parental Warmth and Support

Using data from a large, nationally representative study, we examined the equivalence of measures of maternal and paternal support for European, Chinese, and Filipino American adolescents. We showed that measures of parental support are essentially equivalent for European and Filipino American adolescents but not Chinese American adolescents; among Chinese American adolescents, parental support appears to be interpreted differently or to have different meaning. Results of the study presented in Chapter 3 follow up on these analyses in a study of perceptions of Chinese and European American adolescents and parents. The findings show that Chinese American adolescents report lower warmth from their parents compared to European American adolescents. These reports of warmth are lower perhaps due to conceptual differences in the behaviors that signify warmth, or in the meanings of parental support and warmth for Chinese American adolescents. That is, in daily family life, the differences reported in our study may be indications of ethnically distinct experiences of and meanings associated with warmth and support. This idea is explored further in the fourth chapter, in which we show that sacrifice is a measurably distinct dimension of parental support.

The qualitative study of Chinese and Filipino American girls' and boys' understandings of parental support highlights the tension experienced by first-generation Asian Americans in the United States: they are clearly acculturated to U.S.-based ideas of what "good" parent-adolescent relationships are, enough so that their descriptions of maternal and paternal support shift seamlessly back and forth between dominant cultural and Asian cultural expectations for parent-adolescent relationships. Wu and Chao (2005) show that Chinese American adolescents report a greater disparity between ideal parental warmth and their perceived experiences compared to European Americans. Our focus group discussions provided a rich basis for interpreting their results; the adolescents with whom we spoke discussed these issues as tensions that they negotiated, rather than static disparities between what was "ideal" and "real" for them. Good relationships are characterized by caring communication, but not necessarily the type of communication that these youth consider typical or normative in the dominant cultural context: overt, directly expressive warmth and support. Instead, "you just know" that parents care, and you know this because of the instrumental support and attention provided to these youth through maternal labor and paternal economic provision; this is consistent with descriptions of Asian American family relations in prior research (Uba, 1994; Wu & Chao, 2005), and with the idea that parental sacrifice may be an unspoken part of the family story of immigration, and of ongoing daily instrumental support. Through their discussions, Chinese American adolescent girls in particular struggled with reconciling Western ideals for openness and parental friendship with their experiences and understandings of good parent-adolescent relationships.

Recent research shows that for immigrant Chinese parents, parenting becomes more difficult in the years following immigration: physical discipline is less accepted in the United States, and other parenting practices that were typical in China no longer work in the United States (Qin, 2008). From the adolescents' perspectives, Wu and Chao (2005) argue that Chinese American youth from immigrant families often prefer mainstream American norms of parental warmth to ethnic ones; Asian American adolescents may perceive parents as less warm than their ideals, especially when compared to European American adolescents (see also Kim & Choi, 1994). Our qualitative results extend this work while suggesting something slightly different: the youth in our study acknowledged the differences and tensions that they experienced in day-to-day parent-adolescent relationships. It is not necessarily the case that Asian American adolescents "prefer" mainstream American norms; rather, the adolescents whom we interviewed acknowledged the distinct cultural traditions of their parents while describing the tensions that resulted from growing up in a distinctly different dominant culture. Our studies suggest that adolescents are actively negotiating and interacting in multiple cultures; perhaps adolescents would benefit from an acknowledgement of this dynamic and of their skills. Parke and Buriel (2006) suggest that ethnic minority children could be taught how to interact effectively in dual cultural contexts by encouraging adolescents to understand ethnic as well as dominant cultural norms of parenting (see also Szapocznik & Kurtines, 1993;Wu & Chao, 2005).

This cultural negotiation lends support not only to the contextualized nature of development, but also its dynamic nature; the negotiation of dominant and ethnic cultures adds even greater complexity to the course of development. Youth from immigrant families experience a dual frame of reference involving both the mainstream culture and their ethnic culture, sometimes referred to as "biculturalism." This dual frame of reference contributes to a complexity in the cognitive and social development of youth that current theories of development have not fully captured. Likewise, theories of "biculturalism" have not yet examined the developmental processes underlying the negotiation of a dual frame of reference. Much of the research on biculturalism has been undertaken by social psychologists or sociologists interested in social identity and the notion of cultural frame switching (Tajfel, 1984). However, this research has not explored the dynamic nature of one's social identity and the capacity for cultural frame switching in terms of how they change or become more complex with development. That is, the ability for cultural frame switching requires a degree of socio-cognitive ability that may not begin until children are at least capable of recognizing multiple perspectives. For instance, we know from Piaget's stages of development that children develop the ability to focus on more than one dimension of a problem at a time, a process referred to as "decentering." This often coincides with children also becoming more cognizant of their abilities, and capable of social comparison. Perhaps, at this time, children may also become more conscious of their dual or multi-faceted cultural frames of reference, and may be more critical of one cultural perspective, often their ethnic culture, relative to the other. This developmental appreciation of cultural frame switching then may help us understand how to support children in this process.

Our studies also suggest that the negotiation of ethnic versus dominant cultural frames may vary depending on characteristics of the ethnic culture. A unique contribution of our work is that it highlights what appear to be fundamental differences between Chinese and Filipino American adolescents in the meanings of parental warmth and support. Analyses of maternal and paternal support from the Add Health study show that although the measures are largely equivalent for European and Filipino American adolescents, they are not equivalent for Chinese American adolescents. The underlying meanings of these differences can be inferred from the different ways that Chinese and Filipino American boys and girls described good relationships with mothers and fathers. Among all of the Asian American youth who participated in our study, implicit support was a crucial dimension of parental support: you "just know" that parents care. Combined with results from the fourth chapter, our findings suggest that parental sacrifice may be central to youth's understandings of good relationships and parental support, but the rich descriptions provided by youth in Chapter 5 suggest that "sacrifice" per se is only part of the story. For Chinese American boys, fathers are providers, authority figures, and role models; for Chinese American girls, closeness and affection is not realistic between fathers and daughters. In contrast, for Filipino Americans, boys described fathers as friends as well as providers, and girls described fathers' instrumental support as affectionate. Similarly, while both groups of boys described the instrumental maternal activities that show caring, Filipino American boys also characterized maternal support as including trust and affection. For girls, maternal relationships were based on generational obligations among the Chinese Americans, whereas Filipinas consistently described strictness in their explanations of maternal support and caring.

We have described the Chinese Confucian compared to Filipino Western colonial histories that serve as the basis for the differences in adolescents' descriptions of parental support. For Chinese American adolescents, parent-adolescent relationships are grounded in Confucian understandings of parental authority and intergenerational responsibility and in nonverbal indirect emotional communication styles. Filipino American adolescents also describe an interdependence that is characteristic of Chinese American adolescents, including an emphasis on intergenerational obligation and support. However, in comparison, Filipino family culture has been described as more egalitarian, allowing for affection and closeness, along with a strictness that is based in a history of colonialism that shaped the role of parents as protectors of children, particularly daughters (Espiritu, 2001).

In summary, parental warmth and support clearly matter to Asian American adolescents and their parents. However, the definitions and understandings of warmth and support differ in important ways from European Americans, and between Asian American subgroups. In fact, warmth and support are described in ways that overlap with autonomy and parental control which have traditionally been conceptualized as distinct from or orthogonal to warmth and support (Maccoby & Martin, 1983): perhaps parental warmth and support cannot be defined separately from control as is the case in the West.

Understanding Autonomy and Parental Control

Analyses of the measure of autonomy-granting from the Add Health Study showed that it was not equivalent across any of the three groups; these measures do not capture the dimension of autonomy equally well for European, Chinese, and Filipino adolescents. The comparative study of Chinese and European American parents and adolescents demonstrates that there are distinct parenting beliefs that inform parenting practices, particularly related to parental control and autonomy, and that these beliefs are culturally influenced. Chinese American adolescents and parents endorsed Confucian parental goals and parental control (with the exception of Restrictive Control) more than European American parents. At the same time, results show that Confucian parental goals are not exclusively relevant for Chinese American families. Further, not all results were as expected. There is evidence that for Chinese American parents, contingent autonomy (*guan*) is more strongly linked to child-centered parenting goals than was true for European American parents, whereas the Confucian goals were also linked to this aspect of guan, but for both groups of parents. On the other hand, as expected, the components of guan that involve explaining and expecting obedience were more strongly linked to Confucian parenting goals for Chinese Americans parents than European Americans.

It is unclear from analyses here what role acculturation may play in shaping these results; Chinese American parents are undoubtedly influenced by majority parenting values in the United States, while also maintaining aspects of their ethnic cultural values, and these dual influences may explain some of the unexpected findings from this study. It may be that even when guan is maintained, it is translated to fit within the more dominant child-centered perspective in the United States. We did find that the goals for Confucian and child-centered values were more than twice as highly related for the immigrant Chinese parents than the European American parents. Thus, these sets of goals may become more related or integrated over time as immigrant Chinese parents become acculturated to U.S. values, whereas the European American parents do not begin with such values, but may be exposed to them as they come into contact with the Confucian-based values that some immigrants from Asia may bring with them.

Throughout the focus group discussions of autonomy, Asian American adolescents claimed some degree of independence from parents. We argue that the autonomy they describe is interdependent, which leads us to conclude that researchers should re-consider definitions of independence, particularly when applied to non-European cultural groups. Others have argued that independence in collectivistic cultures is qualitatively different in that it is defined in fundamentally interdependent ways (Markus & Kitayama, 1991). This makes sense: maintaining harmonious relationships is paramount in interdependent cultures. To make independent decisions without concern for the collective would be certain to upend many Asian cultural norms. At the same time, adolescents from cultures characterized by individualism may also experience the intermingling of interdependence with independence, but to a lesser degree than adolescents from interdependent cultures. Anecdotally, it appears that some European American adolescents recognize specific obligations to parents (e.g., to be home on time) and accept the legitimacy of some parental rules; Smetana's work (1988) has shown that European American and African American adolescents distinguish multiple domains of autonomy (much as the Filipino Americans did in this study) and accept the legitimacy of parental authority in particular domains. Thus, it may be useful to reconsider European Americans' experiences and understandings of autonomy through the lens of interdependent-independence as well. For example, in what domains of influence (behavioral, emotional) and in what situations and settings might interdependence characterize independence for European American adolescents?

Differences Between Asian American Groups

Taken together, results from our studies also point to important ethnic group differences among Asian Americans. In developing the measure for parental sacrifice (Chapter 4), items that tapped whether an adolescent felt "grateful" to parents or that she or he "owed a lot" to them appeared as distinctly related to sacrifice for Chinese American youth, but were linked strongly to both sacrifice as well as parental acceptance for Filipino Americans. These items were dropped from further analyses, but the difference between the two ethnic groups is notable. These items are clearly relevant to the broader construct of parental support, but appear to be distinct, particularly for Chinese American adolescents. Western conceptualizations of parental support have not incorporated gratefulness and the concept of owing a debt to parents, yet undoubtedly these are feelings shared by many European American adolescents about their parents. Future research should explore the relevance of these concepts for understanding parenting and parent-adolescent relationships across multiple ethnic groups in the United States.

Results from the Add Health Study (Chapter 2) indicated that a single-factor solution for the measure of autonomy-granting was only equivalent for European and Filipino American boys; all other comparisons failed tests of factorial invariance. Thus, this measure appears to have different meaning across these groups. The focus group data provide some basis for understanding the cultural foundations for these differences. Although Filipino American youth described interdependence, they also acknowledged that their parents do want them to develop independence and to be self-reliant in the future. In contrast, this sentiment was not expressed by Chinese American youth; rather they described their parents' immigrant status as creating opportunities for unexpected independence, or independence that they would not have had were their parents native-born. Chinese Americans described times when they as adolescents had information and language skills that their parents lacked. There were also notable gender differences in the discussions of independence and autonomy. Although all of the boys described responsibility and self-reliance as central to autonomy for Asian American boys, the Filipino American boys specifically noted the importance of financial independence. In girls' discussions of independent decision-making, it was notable that decisions about finances and self-sufficiency were prominent for Filipina girls, whereas discussions about education and college selection were central in discussions by Chinese American girls.

These differences in understandings of adolescent autonomy can be explained by historical differences between Chinese and Filipino culture. Grounded in a history of Western colonialism and Catholicism, Filipino American families may be more egalitarian than patriarchal (Agbayani-Siewert, 1994). This may account for the degree to which Filipino American adolescents described autonomy in interdependent terms, but at the same time indicated that the ultimate goal of their parents was for them to become independent. Notably, the emphasis on financial independence among Filipino American youth is consistent with prior work that has suggested the particular importance of instrumental support among Filipino American families

(Dubrow, Pena, Masten, Sesma, & Williamson, 2001; Fuligni & Pedersen, 2002). In contrast, based in the values of Confucianism, the Chinese Americans appear to be the most collectivist in their worldview (Ho, 1994) in that autonomy, distinct from familial relationships and obligations, simply does not appear to be a primary value. This explains why autonomy is described almost without exception in interdependent and relational terms by Chinese American adolescents.

Beyond Support Versus Autonomy: Supported Autonomy

The emphasis on role obligations and respect for parental authority are greater among adolescents from collectivistic cultures, at least in the immigrant generation (Fuligni & Pedersen, 2002). Values of familial obligation and obedience appear to be the fundamental axes for Asian American adolescents' understandings and interpretations of parental support and autonomy-granting—and the meanings of these values vary between Chinese Americans and Filipino Americans. Ultimately, what is important here is to identify and understand the cultural basis for the observed ethnic group differences. Our results suggest that for Asian Americans, one develops independence in relationships with others, while in the West independence is developed in counter-distinction to primary relationships. In fact, it may be that the distinctions between parental warmth and support and parental control and autonomy-granting are reasonable in the West, but not applicable in the same way in collectivist societies. That is, at least among Chinese Americans, it is possible that the development of autonomy by adolescents is fundamentally relational (or interdependent), defined in part by the support of and relationships with parents, and thus the affective quality of those relations.

By highlighting fundamental conceptual differences based on culture and ethnicity, our work also brings to light possibilities for expanding our understanding of parenting among European Americans. The history of research on parenting practices and behaviors has assumed that support and autonomy-granting are distinct. We suggest that a next step in this field would be to explore the possibilities of an integrated model of parenting in collectivistic—and individualistic—cultures. For example, based on our quantitative and qualitative results from Chinese American adolescents, we question the distinctions made between support and autonomy. Existing studies of ethnically diverse populations that include measures of parental support and control could be used to examine the possibility of a one-dimensional construct of "good parenting" among those from collectivistic cultures. It is plausible that Chinese Americans' notions of parenting, grounded in Confucianism, emphasize the parents' responsibility to socialize the child for harmonious (interdependent) relations with others, and thus is defined as fundamentally control oriented and child-centered (see also Chao, 1994). It is unclear whether this pattern is purely a legacy of traditional Chinese culture or an amalgamation or synthesis of Chinese and U.S. parenting principles that has evolved in the process of acculturation.

Limitations

There are, of course, limitations to the current collection of studies. We began with analyses from the National Longitudinal Study of Adolescent Health, the great benefit of which is our ability to study the reports of parental support and autonomy-granting among European, Chinese, and Filipino American adolescents in a nationally representative sample. These analyses are limited, however, in a number of crucial ways. The measures of parenting, while relevant to the key constructs of parental support and control, were not standard measures familiar in the developmental literature. Thus, the quantitative results are suggestive of ethnic group and gender differences in the conceptualization of these key dimensions of parenting, but the conclusions are limited by our reliance on what is ultimately brief, idiosyncratic measures based on availability. However, it is also the case that the Add Health Study is the largest and most comprehensive ongoing study of adolescent and young adult development in the United States. It continues to offer unique possibilities for the study of human development, family relationships, and health. Given the lasting importance of this data archive, we argue that it is important to understand the cross cultural applicability of the Add Health measures of parenting in spite of these limitations in the measures.

Finally, in the comparative study of Chinese American and European American parents and adolescents, most of the internal consistencies of the scales for parental practices reported by parents were low for both ethnic groups. This may have been due to reductions in the number of items in each scale due to dropped items, or to the need to develop subscales made up of smaller total numbers of items, both of which were necessary in order to maintain comparability in factor structures for adolescents and parents of both ethnic groups. Alternatively, if adolescents from immigrant families use multiple frames of reference, it may be unrealistic to expect consistency in their reports of parenting practices in the first place. Nevertheless, scales with fewer items commonly yield modest or poor internal consistency values. The particularly poor internal consistencies based on *parents*' reports is rather striking, and was only found for the scales for parental *practices*, and not parental goals. Also, parents' and adolescents' reports of parental practices were based on a widely used measure, the CRPBI (i.e., the subscales of Firm versus Lax Control, and of Parental Acceptance). As the alpha coefficients of scales reported by adolescents were adequate to excellent (with the exception of Explains Expectations), it may be that the measurement properties of parental control and warmth scales do indeed differ for adolescents and parents. These findings lend support to arguments that parenting practices may be interpreted very differently by adolescents compared to their parents. These differences in interpretation may be compounded when studying immigrant families. Not only do these families experience the adolescent-parent generational gaps common among all families, they may also experience intergenerational *cultural distancing* due to acculturation differences among family members (Wu & Chao, 2005). Because all the Chinese American *parents* in the study presented in Chapter 3 were first-generation immigrants, the potential intergenerational difference is compounded relative to all the other subgroups. This may make comparability of constructs and measures even more challenging. Further research is needed to better understand the comparability of parenting measures from the perspectives of adolescents and parents in immigrant families.

There are several important limitations to our qualitative study, including the small number of participants, and the limited geographical region from which they were recruited. Because of its historically large immigrant population from the Pacific Rim, Northern California is a strategic location for the study of diversity among Asian Americans. We were able to interview groups of adolescent boys and girls who attended schools with quite different economic status compositions, yet we find striking similarities in discussions of adolescents of the same ethnicity. Nevertheless, the degree to which the responses of these youth are representative of the experiences and understandings of Asian American adolescents in other regions remains to be explored.

The Cultural Bases of Parenting and Adolescent Adjustment

Ultimately our work should inform the literature that is concerned with parenting and adolescent adjustment. We have examined the cultural roots of parenting using distinct methodological approaches, but we have not examined the links between different parenting practices and adolescent adjustment outcomes. A growing literature examines the role of ethnicity and culture in the associations between parenting and adolescent outcomes. Although the notion remains controversial, ample evidence exists to indicate that the effects of parenting practices on child adjustment differ across ethnic groups (Chao, 2001; Lamborn, Mounts, Steinberg, & Dornbusch, 1991; Parke & Buriel, 2006; Shumow & Lomax, 2002; Steinberg, 2001). For example, authoritative parenting is more consistently related to positive adjustment for European American and Hispanic adolescents than for African American and Asian American adolescents (Steinberg, Mounts, Lamborn, & Dornbusch, 1991). Moreover, authoritarian parenting seems to have fewer detrimental effects among minority youth, compared to European American adolescents (Rudy & Grusec, 2001; Steinberg, Lamborn, Darling, & Mounts, 1994), and Asian American adolescents appear to benefit more from permissive parenting than do other adolescents (Lamborn et al., 1991). Yet some research conducted in China and other parts of Asia indicates that authoritative parenting is beneficial and authoritarian parenting is detrimental for adolescents (see review by Sorkhabi, 2005), whereas other research, also conducted in Asia, does not support this pattern (Lau & Cheung, 1987; Leung, Lau, & Lam, 1998; Pearson & Rao, 2003). As an explanation for these conflicting findings, some researchers argue that perhaps Asian parents (specifically Chinese parents), are more authoritative than authoritarian, or else are a combination of both authoritative and authoritarian (Sorkhabi, 2005). However, neither parenting style may adequately capture the most central features of parenting for Asians, including Asian Americans.

We hope that a better understanding of the subtle and diverse meanings of parent-adolescent relationship qualities will provide the basis for further refinement of models of the link among parenting, parent-adolescent relationships, and adolescent adjustment. Analyses that directly examine the effects of parental goals and practices on adolescent adjustment are ultimately needed to determine the consequences of culturally distinct parenting goals and practices for adolescents. Additional studies are needed that examine the cultural processes underlying the effects of parental control and warmth on adolescent adjustment. Ethnic differences in the effects of parenting are often explained in light of cultural distinctions, but these cultural features are often not explicitly examined in studies. Parental beliefs and goals are part of parents' cultural scripts for parenting that may also explain why differential effects for parental control and warmth on adolescents' adjustment have been found across ethnic groups. In particular, we suggest that it is important to measure adolescents' and parents' subjective meanings or interpretations of parenting; these are the products of their cultural frames of reference, and are important for fuller understanding of parenting behavior and adolescent adjustment.

References

Agbayani-Siewert, P. (1994). Filipino American culture and family: Guidelines for practitioners. *Families in Society*, *75*, 429–438.

Chao, R. K. (1994). Beyond parental control and authoritarian parenting style: Understanding Chinese parenting through the cultural notion of training. *Child Development*, *65*, 1111–1119.

Chao, R. K. (2001). Extending research on the consequences of parenting style for Chinese Americans and European Americans. *Child Development*, *72*, 1832–1843.

Durbrow, E. H., Pena, L. F., Masten, A., Sesma, A., & Williamson, I. (2001). Mothers' conceptions of child competence in contexts of poverty: The Philippines, St. Vincent, and the United States. *International Journal of Behavioral Development*, *25*, 438–443.

Espiritu, Y. L. (2001). "We don't sleep around like white girls do": Family, culture, and gender in Filipina American lives. *Journal of Women in Culture and Society*, *26*, 415–440.

Fuligni, A. J., & Pedersen, S. (2002). Family obligation and the transition to young adulthood. *Developmental Psychology*, *38*, 856–868.

Ho, D. Y. F. (1994). Cognitive socialization in Confucian heritage cultures. In P. M. Greenfield & R. R. Cocking (Eds.), *Cross-cultural roots of minority child development* (pp. 285–313). Hillsdale, NJ: Erlbaum.

Kim, U., & Choi, S. H. (1994). Individualism, collectivism, and child development: A Korean perspective. In P. M. Greenfield & R. R. Cocking (Eds.), *Cross-cultural roots of minority child development* (pp. 227–258). Hillsdale, NJ: Lawrence Erlbaum Associates.

Lamborn, S. D., Mounts, N. S., Steinberg, L., & Dornbusch, S. M. (1991). Patterns of competence and adjustment among adolescents from authoritative, authoritarian, indulgent, and neglectful families. *Child Development*, *62*, 1049–1065.

Lau, S., & Cheung, P. C. (1987). Relations between Chinese adolescents' perception of parental control and organization and their perception of parental warmth. *Developmental Psychology*, *23*, 726–729.

Leung, K., Lau, S., & Lam, W. L. (1998). Parenting styles and academic achievement: A cross-cultural study. *Merrill Palmer Quarterly*, *44*, 157–172.

Maccoby, E. E., & Martin, J. A. (1983). Socialization in the context of the family: Parent–child interaction. In E. M. Hetherington (Ed.). *Handbook of child psychology: Vol 4. Socialization, personality, and social development*. New York: Wiley.

Markus, H. R., & Kitayama, S. (1991). Culture and the self: Implications for cognition, emotion, and motivation. *Psychological Review*, *98*, 224–253.

Parke, R. D., & Buriel, R. (2006). Socialization in the family: Ethnic and ecological perspectives. In N. Eisenberg, W. Damon, & R. M. Lerner (Eds.), *Handbook of child psychology: Vol. 3. Social, emotional, and personality development* (6th ed., pp. 429–504). Hoboken, NJ: John Wiley & Sons Inc.

Pearson, E., & Rao, N. (2003). Socialization goals, parenting practices and peer compentence in Chinese and English preschoolers. *Early Child Development and Care. Special Issue: Early Childhood Education in Hong Kong, 173*, 131–146.

Qin, D. B. (2008). Doing well vs. feeling well: Understanding family dynamics and the psychological adjustment of Chinese immigrant adolescents. *Journal of Youth and Adolescence, 37*, 22–35.

Rudy, D., & Grusec, J. E. (2001). Correlates of authoritarian parenting in individualist and collectivist cultures and implications for understanding the transmission of values. *Journal of Cross-Cultural Psychology, 32*, 202–212.

Shumow, L., & Lomax, R. (2002). Parental efficacy: Predictor of parenting behavior and adolescent outcomes. *Parenting: Science & Practice, 2*, 127.

Smetana, J. G. (1988). Adolescents' and parents' conceptions of parental authority. *Child Development, 59*, 321–335.

Sorkhabi, N. (2005). Applicability of Baumrind's parent typology to collective cultures: Analysis of cultural explanations of parent socialization effects. *International Journal of Behavioral Development, 29*, 552–563.

Steinberg, L. (2001). We know some things: Parent and adolescent relationships in retrospect and prospect. *Journal of Research on Adolescence, 11*, 1.

Steinberg, L., Lamborn, S. D., Darling, N., & Mounts, N. S. (1994). Over-time changes in adjustment and competence among adolescents from authoritative, authoritarian, indulgent, and neglectful families. *Child Development, 65*, 754–770.

Steinberg, L., Mounts, N., Lamborn, S., & Dornbusch, S. (1991). Authoritative parenting and adolescent adjustment across varied ecological niches. *Journal of Research on Adolescence, 1*, 19–36.

Szapocznik, J., & Kurtines, W. M. (1993). Family psychology and cultural diversity: Opportunities for theory, research, and application. *American Psychologist, 48*, 400–407.

Tajfel, H. (1984). Intergroup relations, social myths and social justice in social psychology. In H. Tajfel (Ed.), *The social dimension: European developments in social psychology* (pp. 695–715). Cambridge: Cambridge University Press.

Uba, L. (1994). *Asian Americans: Personality patterns, identity, and mental health.* New York: Guilford Press.

Wu, C. X., & Chao, R. K. (2005). Intergenerational cultural conflicts for Chinese American youth with immigrant parents: Norms of parental warmth and the consequences. *International Journal of Behavioral Development, 29*, 516–523.

Subject Index

A

Acculturation, 59, 101, 112, 122, 124–125
Adjustment, 1–4, 7, 32, 62–63, 118, 126–127
Adolescent independence, 102, 109, 112
Adolescent interpretation and understanding, 61
Autonomy, 2–3, 10–11, 18–20, 22, 24–26, 28–33, 38, 41–42, 44–52, 55–59, 79, 81, 84, 101–115, 118, 121–125

B

Behavioral control, 3, 11, 38–39, 41–43, 46–47, 50–51, 55–56, 58–59

C

Chinese American, 2, 4–11, 17–25, 27–33, 37–59, 61–62, 65–68, 72, 75, 79–99, 101–115, 117–125
Chinese immigrants, 47, 58, 75, 101
Confucian parental goals, 56, 121–122
Contingent autonomy, 38–39, 42, 44–49, 52, 55–57, 59, 101, 108–109, 112–113, 122
Contingent terms, 112
Cross-ethnic equivalence, 19, 29
Cross-ethnic invariance (similarity), 29
Cultural
  meaning, 1, 2, 5, 10, 37, 39, 74, 79
  processes, 2, 10, 56, 59, 64, 118, 127
Cultural differences, 2, 4, 10, 18–19, 61, 74, 79, 117
Culturally sensitive measures, 75
Cultural meaning, 1–2, 5, 10, 37, 39, 74, 79
Cultural perspective, 18, 120
Culture
  cultural assumptions, 117
  cultural beliefs, 10, 18
  cultural practices, 63
  cultural representations (of families), 117

D

Daily family experiences, 97
Day to day decisions, 112
Discipline, 4, 6, 98, 119

E

Emotional closeness, 87–88, 97
Equivalence of measures, 29, 65, 74, 118
Ethnic differences, 1, 4, 7–10, 18–19, 30, 44, 49, 55–57, 62, 79, 97–98, 102, 127
Ethnic group differences, 47
European Americans, 1, 4–6, 10–11, 17–19, 21–22, 24–25, 28–30, 37–59, 61, 74–75, 97, 101, 117, 119, 121–122, 124
Explains obedience, 42, 44–48, 52–59

F

Family
  interactions, 117
  relationships, 8, 62, 99, 117–118, 125
Family role obligations, 112
Fathers, 2, 7, 21–22, 27–28, 32, 40, 43, 67–68, 81–82, 87–90, 92–99, 110, 115, 120–121
Filipino American, 2, 7–12, 17–33, 61–76, 79–99, 101–115, 118–125

G

Gender differences, 7, 24, 123, 125
Guan, 41, 52–53

S.T. Russell et al. (eds.), *Asian American Parenting and Parent-Adolescent Relationships,* Advancing Responsible Adolescent Development,
DOI 10.1007/978-1-4419-5728-3, © Springer Science+Business Media, LLC 2010

I
Immigrant, 3–5, 10–11, 33, 37–59, 61–65, 68, 74–75, 88, 97, 101–102, 111–112, 119–120, 122–126
Independence, 101–115
Instrumental support, 5, 64, 74, 85, 90, 97, 113, 119, 121, 123
Interdependence, 7, 101–115, 121–123

L
Life goals, 102, 107, 112

M
Maternal relationship, 82–83, 121
Maternal support, 22, 24–27, 29–31, 113, 121
Measurement equivalence, 10, 17–33, 62, 65
Measurement invariance, 66, 72–74
Media, 3, 117
Mothers, 2, 5, 7, 9, 31, 57, 68, 81–87, 89–92, 95–99, 105–106, 113–115, 120

N
National Longitudinal Study of Adolescent Health (Add Health Study), 19–20, 125

O
Openness, 88, 97, 119

P
Parent-adolescent
  closeness, 97
  communication, 27–28, 30, 83, 87–89, 91–99, 121
  quality, 79–99
  relationship, 1–12, 19, 33, 59, 61, 75, 79–80, 82, 96–97, 101, 112, 117–127
Parent-adolescent relationships, 1–12, 19, 33, 59, 61, 75, 79–80, 82, 96–97, 101, 112, 117–127
  quality, 79–99
Parental
  authoritarian, 4–6, 126
  authoritative, 1, 4, 6, 126
  autonomy-granting, 2, 32, 81, 101, 111, 118, 121, 123–125
  behaviors, 6, 10, 18, 37
  beliefs, 2, 10, 37–59, 127
  concerns, 5–6, 112
  control, 2–6, 11, 17–18, 37–39, 41, 56, 58, 61, 75, 99, 101, 121–122, 124–125, 127
  goals
    child-centered (contingent autonomy), 43–45, 47–50, 52–53, 55–58
    confucian, 47–50, 52–58, 122
  measures, 44
  monitoring, 3
  parenting, 1–12, 17–33, 57, 80, 117–127
  perspectives, 112
  practices, 37–59, 61, 125
  preferences, 102, 107, 112–114
  styles, 1–3, 5, 11, 98, 121
  support, 2–3, 5, 8, 10–11, 17–20, 24, 26–27, 29–33, 61–76, 79–81, 98, 102, 117–121, 123–125
  warmth, 3, 5–6, 11, 21, 39, 42, 46, 61, 79, 118–121, 124
Parent-child relationships, 1, 10–11, 18, 31–32, 64, 114, 117
Parenting, 1–12, 17–33, 57, 80, 117–127
Paternal relationship, 82, 97
Psychosocial adjustment, 1–2

R
Relational terms, 102, 124

S
Sacrifice, 61–76
Socialization
  family (family socialization), 2, 64

Breinigsville, PA USA
11 May 2010
237748BV00002B/17/P